Managing Productivity

Managing Productivity

Joel E. Ross
Professor of Management
Florida Atlantic University

Reston Publishing Company, Inc.
A Prentice-Hall Company
Reston, Virginia

Library of Congress Cataloging in Publication Data

Ross, Joel E.
  Managing productivity.

  Includes bibliographical references and index.
  1. Industrial productivity. 2. Industrial management.
I. Title.
HD56.R67   658.4   76-30558
ISBN 0-87909-459-1

© 1977 by
Reston Publishing Company, Inc.
A *Prentice-Hall Company*
Reston, Virginia 22090

10   9   8   7   6

Printed in the United States of America

Contents

PREFACE / ix

1   PRODUCTIVITY: THE CENTRAL TASK OF THE MANAGER / 1

The Challenge / 2
The Reality / 2
The People Problem: Who's to Blame? / 3
The Decreasing Role of Technology / 4
The Leverage of Management / 5
The Answer: Better Management / 6
Check Your Productivity Quotient / 8

2   MANAGING PRODUCTIVITY: A SYSTEMS APPROACH / 11

Focus on Results / 12
Organizational Integration / 15
Organizing for Results / 16
The Iceberg Analogy / 18
A System for Managing Productivity / 19
Check Your Concepts of Productivity Management / 21

3   MANAGING SUBORDINATES: MOTIVATION AND
     PRODUCTIVITY, JOB DEVELOPMENT, AND
     APPRAISAL / 23

     Motivation and Productivity / 25
     Factors Affecting Productivity / 26
     Job Development / 29
     Appraisal / 34
     Managing Subordinates: Check Your Readiness / 40

4   MANAGING SUBORDINATES: DEVELOPMENT
     AND COMMUNICATION / 41

     Developing Subordinates / 42
     Communication / 46
     Checklist for Subordinate Development and Communication / 53

5   MANAGING SUBORDINATES: DELEGATION
     AND CONTROL, LEADERSHIP STYLE, AND
     ORGANIZATIONAL STYLE / 55

     Delegation / 56
     Control / 58
     Leadership Style / 61
     Organizational Style / 72
     Evaluate Your Readiness for Control and Leadership / 77

6   MANAGEMENT BY OBJECTIVES: THE SYSTEM
     FOR ACHIEVING RESULTS / 79

     Objectives / 81
     Hierarchy of Objectives / 81
     MBO as a System for Getting Results / 84
     Summary: Making MBO Work / 97
     Are You Ready for MBO? / 100

7   PROBLEM DEFINITION AND ANALYSIS / 103

     What is a Problem? / 104
     The Process of Problem Definition and Analysis / 105
     Steps in the Problem Definition and Analysis Process / 109
     Problem Definition / 109
     Problem Analysis / 112
     People Problems / 117

Problem Analysis as a Way of Managerial Life / 118
Case Study: Office Systems, Inc. / 119
Check Your Problem-Solving Readiness / 125

8 DECISION MAKING / 127

The Concept of Rational Choice / 128
The Decision-Making Process / 131
Decision Making and Problem Solving: Summary / 146
Case Study: Office Systems, Inc., (continued) / 148
Checklist: Can You Make a Good Decision? / 151

9 ACTION PLANNING / 153

Top Management Planning is Not Action Planning / 155
The Action Plan / 155
Summary / 166
Action Check for Action Planning / 167

10 MANAGING YOUR TIME / 169

Needed: A Strategy for Time Management / 171
Ten Top Time Wasters / 171
Ten Solutions for Time Wasters / 175
Time Management Strategy: Identify Time Wasters / 180
Time Management: A Plan / 180
Summary: Time Management Concepts / 183

INDEX / 187

Preface

The need to improve productivity in organizations today is evident to everyone; national leaders, chief executives, and individual managers alike. Better management practice at all levels in the organization is the method increasingly accepted as the single best way to improve productivity. The means by which individual managers can achieve productivity through improved management are not as obvious.

As a management practitioner, author, teacher, and consultant, my growing concern is that the way we teach management is correlated with the shortcomings of current management practices. This book discusses solutions to three of these basic shortcomings.

First, there is the growing proliferation of topics, techniques, and theories. These range from time management to decision making, from communications to basic supervision, from managing conflict to leadership styles, and so on. All of these topics are important but there has been no integrating framework that relates one topic to the other and to the whole. Hence it is difficult for a manager or a student of management to build a logical, integrated body of knowledge and practice. I think this book helps to deal with that shortcoming by integrating the most important and basic management techniques around a system of *results management* with a central theme of *productivity*.

A second problem has been the lack of an applied approach that tells the user how this or that topic can be applied on the job. I have tried to guide the reader so the idea or technique can be put to work for immediate improvement in productivity on the job.

A third and final shortcoming in teaching applied management has been that they stop short of converting the idea into action. After you have learned "decision making" what do you then do with the decision? After you have learned "management by objectives" what do you do with your objective, once established? I have tried to *operationalize* the topics of this book by relating them to the necessary implementing procedure of *action planning* and the related disciplines of problem solving and decision making. Finally, all the topics of management are related to the central theme of productivity.

My thanks go to the thousands of university students who increasingly demand reality in management education and to the thousands of supervisors and managers in seminars who have found these ideas and methods to be valuable in improving their own productivity.

Joel Ross

Managing Productivity

1

Productivity

The Central Task of the Manager

The Challenge
The Reality
The People Problem: Who's to Blame?
The Decreasing Role of Technology
The Leverage of Management
The Answer: Better Management
Check Your Productivity Quotient

By almost any measure the productivity picture in the United States can only be described as dismal. Although the American worker remains slightly ahead in the productivity race, the gap is closing rapidly as the rest of the industrial world accelerates. The capital-intensive United States, home of industrial engineering and the assembly line, production planning and the computer, has recently witnessed its first productivity decline in output per working hour in three decades. Japan and the leading nations of Western Europe bettered us in rate of growth as we fell to ninth place among the dozen leading industrial nations in the rate of productivity increase.

Reversing this trend is of significant concern to each of us. At the *national* level it is the best way to stop inflation and improve real income. At the *company* level it is the only way to reduce costs and improve profits. And for the *individual* managers, improving their own productivity is central to their jobs. For each, it means the way to increased responsibility, satisfaction, and growth.

THE CHALLENGE

Getting better results by productivity improvement is the most important task of all managers, whatever their level in the company. Many middle-level managers and supervisors believe that this is the concern of top management and only that group is responsible. This is not so. Without some *measurable* productivity objective, neither the organization nor the individual manager have a sense of direction. Planning, if done at all, proceeds without any definable goal. Control cannot be exercised because there is no method for measuring performance against plan. The extent to which resources are made productive becomes the primary test of the manager's ability as well as the standard by which we can compare the performance of organizations.

Peter Drucker, the popular management writer, says that making work productive and the worker achieve is the major dimension of the management task. This dimension is also a challenge. It is a challenge because productivity improvement has no mature body of knowledge or group of tested methods, nor does there exist a clearly defined yardstick by which it can be measured. Add to this the accelerating social change and the uncertain knowledge of human motivation and we do indeed face a challenge.

THE REALITY

Productivity is somewhat like the weather; many people are talking about it but few are doing anything. If you asked the question: "Who's in charge of productivity?" the typical company would reply, "Nobody!"

Richard C. Gerstenberg, former chairman of General Motors, says he is astonished at how few major companies "even know what productivity is." In a 1975 survey of 6,000 business managers, the American Management Associations found serious worry over productivity, but two thirds of the respondents in the survey reported their companies were making no special effort to evaluate executive productivity.[1]

Some industries are particularly lax in efficiency. This appears to be higher than average in service industries which make up about fifty percent of our gross national product. When you combine this with the "service" or overhead departments of other types of business you have an enormous sector that is not being gauged by any value-added measure. A senior executive in a large insurance company says, "The service industries cannot answer some of the basic questions relating to their operations. We spent three years installing our information system but we can't tell how much it cost since we don't have a cost accounting system to tell us. However, as slow as the insurance industry is, it appears that the banking industry is still behind us."

Government agencies and industries regulated by the government come in for their share of criticism. Twenty years ago the railroads guaranteed delivery of a head of lettuce from California to the East in six days. Today it takes eleven days. It is estimated that a rail car is moving under load only seven percent of the time. Productivity varies by as much as one thousand percent in some government operations.

During the most recent period for which data are available, productivity in Japan increased at five times the rate of the United States. Japanese government expenditures on productivity improvement are over six times the amount spent by the U.S. government, despite the fact that our federal budget is five times larger than Japan's.

THE PEOPLE PROBLEM: WHO'S TO BLAME?

What's the problem? Whatever your personal view, you can probably find support for your conclusion. Each of the causes listed has come in for its share of the blame.

Many executives think that militant *labor unions* restrict improvements in productivity. No doubt this feeling has some validity. In some companies it appears that an imbalance of power between management and labor has occurred. In some extreme cases unions may have as much to say about day-to-day operations as management. One frustrated official remarked, "Workers believe that since they come to the plant forty hours per week they can't be expected to work too!"

[1] Mildred E. Katzell, *Productivity: The Measure and the Myth*. New York: Amacom, 1975.

The *government* is everybody's whipping boy. It is said that efficiency is being stifled by regulations. Additionally, many companies complain that the U.S. government, unlike governments in other countries, does little to encourage private investment in plants and equipment, nor does it take additional measures to support free enterprise. While there may be some truth in these complaints on a company basis, they are hardly justification for individual managers to become lax.

The rise of the *service industries* has changed the "blue collar blues" to the "white collar blues." It is said that a growing proportion of the work force are "knowledge workers" and since it is difficult to define the output of this type of worker, it is difficult to measure their productivity. Moreover, some manual workers have adopted self-defeatist attitudes because they perceive themselves as second class citizens.

Some managers blame *egalitarianism* for the "the world owes me a living" attitude of some workers. This accelerating philosophy is causing near-apoplexy in some board rooms.[2] Broadly defined, the movement seeks equality of condition—more equal distribution of income, housing, consumer goods, and social status—as well as equality of rights. The modern egalitarians have placed their hostility squarely at the door of the corporation and have demanded government intervention to assure equality. Opponents of the movement point to the management and financial fiasco in New York City as an example of the likely consequences of a welfare state.

THE DECREASING ROLE OF TECHNOLOGY

During a visit to India in 1975 I was able to visit several cities and talk to many managing directors of Indian firms. I was constantly amazed at the low level of application of technology except in the very largest firms. From my hotel room in Bombay I observed with interest as construction of a modern oceanfront hotel proceeded into the thirty-sixth month, half-completed. Typical work methods could be illustrated by dozens of "carriers" who spent their working day stacking a load of eight bricks onto the top of their head and walking a hundred yards to the construction site where they queued for unloading into a muscle-powered lift. It wouldn't take an industrial engineer to calculate that one wheelbarrow, a piece of capital-intensive equipment in India, would replace about ten human workers.

The potential for muscle leverage that can be achieved by technology

---

[2] For a disturbing scenario of this movement, see "Egalitarianism: Mechanisms for Redistributing Income," *Business Week*, December 8, 1975. Also "Egalitarianism: The Corporation As Villian," *Business Week*, December 15, 1975.

such as the wheelbarrow is easily understood and applied by both worker and manager alike in the United States. During the twentieth century we have become the most capital-intensive nation in the world. Our capital resources have combined with innovative engineering to provide us with a technology base that is unsurpassed. We have traditionally depended upon technology to solve everything from defense needs and environmental problems to our increased standard of living. The remaining two components of increased productivity, labor and management, have played a secondary role.

This emphasis is changing fast. Some say we've gone about as far as we can go until the human element catches up with technology. The 3M chief executive, Harry Heltzer, reflects this conclusion in his comment: "You can't press the button any harder and make the automated equipment run any faster. In a rising cost spiral you've just got to find ways of pressing it more intelligently." In other words, working harder is not the total answer; we've got to work "smarter" too.

In the American Management Associations survey mentioned previously, greater capital investment ranked thirteenth on a list of factors considered very important in terms of influencing an organization's productivity. In the survey of 6,000 managers, only twenty seven percent ranked capital investment as very important and only thirty five percent ranked technology as very important. The overwhelming choice for improved productivity was *better management*.

THE LEVERAGE OF MANAGEMENT

Despite the popular belief that the biggest roadblock to productivity is people, (particularly labor), the evidence seems to indicate otherwise.

Most people understand and appreciate the principle of muscle or mechanical leverage. Mental leverage is not so widely appreciated or understood. To demonstrate this for yourself, close your eyes and try to multiply five numbers (e.g., 367×79) in your head without benefit of paper and pencil. Most people give up after ten or fifteen minutes. Yet with the aid of simple technology such as a pencil and paper I am able to perform the calculation in fifteen seconds. With a hand-held calculator, another generation of technology, the time is reduced to three seconds. Consider yet a higher level of technology:

> In 1952 it cost $1.26 to do 100,000 mutiplications on an IBM computer. Today, they can be done for a penny. Multiplications have gone from 2000 a second to more than 2 million a second today.

> IBM Advertisement (1976)

Unfortunately, the potential for mental leverage with the computer, a special case of technology, goes largely unrealized.

Now consider these questions: (1) Is it likely that the application of good management can provide increased leverage to operational improvements and hence to productivity increases? (2) Can we consider the management of productivity a special case of technology? The answer to both of these questions must be in the affirmative.

The improvements resulting from better management are not so easily identified and quantified, therefore the multiplier effect is often overlooked. However, we do know that failure to apply good management can result in disaster.[3]

THE ANSWER: BETTER MANAGEMENT

Management consultant John Patton, who has been studying the subject for thirty years, says, "Declining productivity is not entirely the fault of organized labor . . . it is not entirely the fault of our patronizing, interfering government . . . it is not entirely the fault of the shifting attitudes of our younger generation . . . the real fault lies squarely at the feet of management, for not seizing the initiative to take remedial action."

A number of productivity studies make it clear that there is room for blame across the board. The productivity problem is no more the fault of the production line worker than that of the middle manager or supervisor or even the president of the company. To quote former chairman Gerstenberg of General Motors again, "Better productivity results from better management."

If this is the case, why do so many people overlook the leverage potential of improved management? It is probably because the managers themselves so frequently overlook it or they are unaware of the techniques and methods at their disposal.

Productivity—the ratio of some measure of output to some measure of input—a difficult measure at best, is usually attributed to the improved efficiency of some specific resource such as capital, money, materials, or technology. For example, one familiar output–input measure is miles per gallon of gasoline. We use this measure not as a gauge of the efficiency of the gasoline but as an indicator of the efficiency of the car's performance. We overlook the accumulated technology and capital that has been *managed* by the petroleum companies. More recently, the energy shortage has demanded increased efficiency (productivity) of automobile engines. We have assumed that this increase is solely a function of en-

[3] See Joel E. Ross and Michael Kami, *Corporate Management in Crisis: Why the Mighty Fall.* Englewood Cliffs, N.J.: Prentice-Hall, Inc., 1973.

gineering design whereas it resulted from the volume and quality of other inputs that were planned, organized, and controlled by *management*. And here I mean the process of management and not a group of persons.

There exists a paradox among managers. On the one hand there is a growing consensus that the most important factors in improving productivity depend on management: better planning, more effective job procedures, better communications, more effective human resource policies, improved decision making, and so on. On the other hand there is a reluctance to tackle the job. Managers at all levels need to roll up their sleeves and get to work.

Top level managers have two tasks. First they must develop and disseminate a strategy that will guide each member of the organization in a unified sense of direction. They must answer the questions: What kind of company do we want to be? What is our purpose and mission? What is our product/market scope and our competitive edge? What are our major objectives and the plans to achieve them?

The second task of top management is to determine the necessary investment to make in productivity. They have done it for technology and they have done it for marketing. It is now time to make a commitment to productivity. Part of this investment should be in management development.

Individual managers and supervisors need to stop thinking in terms of performing activities and think instead in terms of results. They must think in terms of motivating subordinates and managing work. Objectives must be achieved through action plans arrived at in an orderly manner through better problem solving and decision making.

It is the purpose of this book to provide the framework to begin the practical application of the means to improve productivity through the performance of these tasks of management.

CHECK YOUR
PRODUCTIVITY QUOTIENT

	Yes	*No*
1. Does your company have a productivity improvement program?	( )	( )
Is someone in charge?	( )	( )
Is there a formal structure?	( )	( )
Are managers at all levels involved?	( )	( )

A *no answer means you should get organized for productivity.*

2. Have you as an individual manager taken any specific action to improve productivity?	( )	( )

If the answer is no you should think through your responsibilities in terms of productivity.

3. Do you find yourself blaming others for lack of productivity improvement?	( )	( )
Labor	( )	( )
Government	( )	( )
Social Change	( )	( )

A *yes answer means you should check out your management style as the primary avenue for increasing productivity.*

4. Do you believe that your job is not subject to productivity measurement because you are a supervisor, knowledge worker, or that your job is too "creative" to measure?	( )	( )

If the answer is yes you should think in terms of getting some form of yardstick to measure the results of your job.

5. Can you demonstrate specifically how better management can improve productivity in:

Your company?	( )	( )
Your job?	( )	( )

A *no answer indicates a need for a review of basic management principles.*

6. Has a commitment been made to improved
productivity through improved management
development:

By your company?   ( ) ( )
By you?   ( ) ( )

If the answer is no; read on!

2

Managing Productivity

A Systems Approach

Focus on Results
Organizational Integration
Organizing for Results
The Iceberg Analogy
A System for Managing Productivity
Check Your Concepts of Productivity
    Management

Synergism is the notion that the sum of the parts is greater than the whole—2 + 2 = 5—the output of the total organization can be enhanced if the component parts can be integrated. This managerial concept has now reached maturity.

There is now almost universal agreement that the primary job of a manager is to create a whole that is larger than the sum of its parts, an organizational entity that turns out more than the sum of the resources put into it. In business this is termed *profit*. In the public sector it may be called *surplus*. All organizations must add some value to the inputs they receive. Likewise, individual managers must add value to the resources that are placed into their custody for processing into outputs.

This basic notion comprises the central theme of the systems approach to management. It is based on two fundamental concepts:

1. Focus on the output—the results of the system

2. Integration of the parts or subsystems of the organization

These two concepts provide the framework around which we can develop *a system of management for productivity improvement.*

FOCUS ON RESULTS

Consider the concept of a system shown conceptually in Figure 2–1. Any system, whether business, mechanical, electrical, or biological has three components: input, processor, and output. Consider also these characteristics of system operation:

1. Inputs are received into the system.

2. The inputs are processed by various activities (organizational subsystems) carried on in the processor.

3. The activities add value to the inputs and provide an output.

4. Productivity of the activities is measured by the ratio of the output to the input. This rate must be a positive value.

Despite the simplicity of the systems concept and its applicability to business and government operations, it is often overlooked by managers who focus on activities rather than on results.

Managers can sometimes be characterized by which part of the "system" they emphasize: (1) input, (2) activity, or (3) output.

1. The *input* managers or employees are recognizable by their dedication to organization input. They delight in providing data for variance reports on sales or quality control. They perform a careful scrutiny of supporting documents for expense accounts; their emphasis is on paperwork

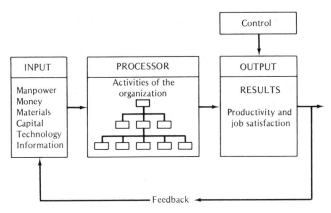

Figure 2-1. The Organization as a System
Note: The basic measure of productivity for any organization or subsystem thereof is simple. It is a ratio of some measure of output to some measure of input. In business, we seek a positive "contribution value" for the processor, i.e., output should be greater than input. For more detail, *see* Leon Greenberg, *A Practical Guide to Productivity Measurement.* Washington, D.C.: Bureau of National Affairs, 1973.

and the maintenance of records. They are the guardian of company rules and procedures but are unconcerned or unaware of any relationship between their own input and results. The means become the end. They emphasize form and administration (doing things right) rather than process and management (doing the right things).

2. The *activity* manager is most in evidence and the majority of us can be labeled this way. We give our attention to activities and not results. The accountant focuses on preparation of the cost report rather than on reduction of overhead costs. The sales representative thinks of calling on customers, not optimizing the profitability of the product/customer mix. The engineer is concerned only with the technical specifications of design without regard to cost, value analysis, or competitive considerations.

Few managers see their responsibilities in terms of *results*. When asked to define their managerial role they will reply with such platitudes as: . . . "improve the operations" . . . "supervise the assembly unit" . . . "meet the needs of the customer" . . . "keep maintenance costs down" . . . "stay within the budget" . . . "have the right person at the right place at the right time."

All of us have witnessed everyday cases where results are being impeded by "activity focus" in such operations as the retail store or the hospital. All too frequently the salesperson in the store is bent on complying with company policy and carrying on busywork related to paper procedures rather than getting results through the real job of selling and servicing the customer. In the typical hospital the nurse is deskbound under a flood of paper to the detriment of the real job of patient care.

An axiomatic principle of bureaucracy is that focus on activity has a perfectly logical structure to those who are trapped in it. So it is with the person who is trapped in activity rather than in results. The activity may be logical to the individual, but to an outsider the individual or organization is wasteful and perhaps unreliable.

There is an old story that tells of three bricklayers on a construction job who were asked by their foreman what they were doing. The first replied, "I am making a living." The second bricklayer said simply, "I am laying bricks." The third announced proudly, "I am building the best office building in town." The third bricklayer, of course, was the one who focused on results.[1]

3. The *output* (output is henceforth called results) managers are easy to spot. They call for results loudly and frequently but are never specific about what is expected. They demand results in such terms as: "we've got to get on the ball around here" or "let's sharpen up the operations" or "get busy . . . move it." Although they are concerned with production, they don't define it and consequently their supervisory style consists of close control of subordinates, making sure they are kept busy. The subordinates, in turn, are frustrated and demotivated. They don't know what's expected.

The Results-Oriented Manager

This type of manager views the department, unit, or shop in terms of the results expected from it. Moreover, they are specific in the definition of these results and what value is to be added to the resources of the unit. Productivity must be represented by a positive output/input ratio. Activities are conducted for the sole purpose of achieving a definable result.

These managers don't say, "sharpen up the operations" but ask instead, "can we achieve a scrap rate of three percent?" They don't say "improve the cost control report" but instead say, "let us design by May 1st a cost report that will identify, by line and product, forecasted labor variance in order to reduce direct labor costs to the budgeted amount."

Their supervisory style is one that balances the need for production with the need for motivation and job satisfaction. Indeed, they know that the achievement of results can be a strong motivator.

---

[1] For a different twist on this story, consider the reply by the foreman to the third bricklayer, "You are fired because you don't know the objective. We are building a warehouse."

ORGANIZATIONAL INTEGRATION

The systems approach has as its second major dimension the integration of organizational subsystems in order to optimize the output of the whole. To say that most companies have something less than synergism is an understatement. As one frustrated chief executive remarked: "Sales is selling a product that Engineering can't design, that Manufacturing can't make, and to customers that Finance won't approve for credit."

Lack of integration can best be illustrated by the traditional "confrontation" between Sales and Manufacturing. Sales wants to sell one of each color delivered this afternoon, and Manufacturing wants to ship one million unit lots, all black, when they are ready. There are constant problems regarding capacity, product mix, lead time, order backlogs, over or under scheduling, over or under booking, and back schedules.

When this situation is at its worst, Manufacturing understates capacity and overstates lead times in self-defense. Sales will guard against Manufacturing conservatism by overbooking and accepting orders after the expiration of lead time. There is little effective communication about the status of items in process. Production planning becomes item expediting—a reflex spasm triggered by the latest complaint of the highest sales executive.

Much of the organizational inflexibility and antiproductive behavior can be traced to the way in which the typical company is organized. In most cases they have a traditional, classical organization structure. It continues to be the most common corporate and government structure in use today. It inhibits productivity.

The Classical Bureaucracy

The four key pillars of classical organization structure are: (1) specialization of work (departmentation), (2) span of control (nobody supervises over five or six subordinates), (3) unity of command (nobody works for more than one boss), and (4) the chain of command (the authority hierarchy). The manager determines what work activities and tasks are necessary to get the job done, writes job descriptions, and organizes people into groups and assigns them to superiors. Standards of performance are then established. Operations are controlled through a reporting system. The whole structure takes on the shape of a pyramid such as illustrated in Figure 2–2.

How do we arrive at a bureaucratic, pyramidal structure? The answer lies in an understanding of how a company grows and develops. In the beginning, communication is simple and effective because activities and communication channels are few in number, but as operations grow in

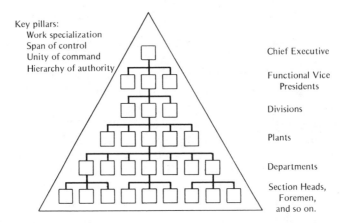

Key pillars:
    Work specialization
    Span of control
    Unity of command
    Hierarchy of authority

Chief Executive

Functional Vice
    Presidents

Divisions

Plants

Departments

Section Heads,
    Foremen,
    and so on.

Figure 2–2.   The Classical Organization

size and communication becomes more complex, proper coordination and direction demands written directives and procedures. Communication is between offices, not people. More growth means more complexity, and that calls for more policies, procedures, and further formalization. In time, the proliferation of systems, procedures, and regulations demands greater departmentation and more staff people to coordinate operations.

A characteristic of the pyramidal structure is tight control over authority and its delegation. Managers tend to view themselves as "boss" and their authority becomes their security blanket.

Criticizing the systems, formality, and controls of the bureaucracy is getting to be a profitable vocation. Witness *Parkinson's Law*, *The Peter Principle*, and *Up the Organization*. Many of these criticisms have a basis in truth, but to abandon the classical structure in favor of some "free form" or other approach to organizational design is not only unwise, but unlikely! The challenge is to modify the pyramid in order to minimize the bureaucratic disadvantages of work specialization and hierarchical authority. We need to crack the bureaucracy while at the same time maintaining its basic form.

ORGANIZING FOR RESULTS

The systems approach can increase productivity by modifying the restrictive characteristics of the bureaucracy. Part of the problem has been that we have always organized by activities and tasks—basic processes of labor specialization and classical organization theory—rather than by results. Just as the industrial engineer should question the final product before questioning the work process, the manager should question the results expected before designing the tasks and activities of the organization structure. Incidentally, this is a major reason for resistance to organizational analysts and industrial engineers; people can't identify with the output they are seeking.

In principle and in practice the systems approach helps to improve synergism. Instead of jockeying for position, or attempting to push special interests and arguing all the time, the crux of organizational disputes shifts from arguing about process (activities) to one of deciding on the best course of action to get results. They shift from quibbling about what is our present latitude and longitude to fruitful discussions about where we should head. Traditional organization theory is concerned with the organization of authority. The systems approach is concerned with organizing responsibility and getting on with the job.

Perhaps the best way to demonstrate how the systems approach (focus on results) can improve the classical structure is to compare the charges leveled at the bureaucracy against the advantages of a results management approach. This is done in Table 2–1.

Table 2–1. Comparison of the Classical Organization and Results Management

Charges Leveled at the Classical Organization	Advantages of Results Management
Too mechanistic. Too structured to adapt to change.	Dynamic. Permits flexibility as system adapts to change in output requirements.
Formality hinders communications.	Communications based on results, not procedure or directive.
Inhibits innovation.	Encourages innovation. People seek innovative achievement goals.
Pays the job and not the man.	Rewards based on appraisal by results.
Relies on coercive control.	Self-control.
Job-defensive behavior encourages make-work.	All work devoted to goal achievement based on results.
Organization goals not compatible with goals of organization members.	Individual and organization goals are the same: production.
Out of date with human needs.	Meets basic human need for self-actualization.

THE ICEBERG ANALOGY

We know that approximately ninety percent of an iceberg's volume is under water and hidden from the observer's view. Only a small portion is visible. To the uninformed traveler, only the visible portion seems to exist. However, a seasoned sailor seeks to account for the hidden part below the surface.

An organization is somewhat like an iceberg. The novice, or the seat-of-the-pants manager, sees only visible organizational potential and usually adopts a managerial style that is heavily dependent on tradition and personal experience. He likes to describe himself as "informal" and feels that popular management techniques are nothing more than common sense descriptions of what he does instinctively. He runs things "by the book" and depends on formal authority and standard procedures. He is the classical manager.

What the classical manager frequently overlooks is the unreleased potential in the organization for improved productivity through more modern management methods. If he could visualize the potential for improved productivity, both he and the organization would benefit.

The potential for improved productivity is significant but is being suppressed by classical techniques of organization and management. The analogy between the iceberg and the organization is shown in Figure 2–3. The solution lies in the adoption of a systems approach to managing productivity.

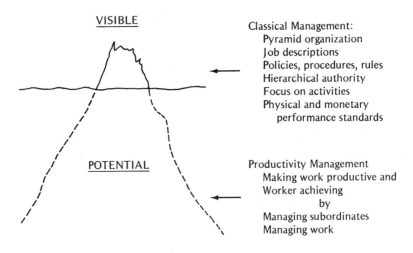

Figure 2–3.   The Organization as an Iceberg

A SYSTEM FOR MANAGING PRODUCTIVITY

We are now ready to outline the framework of a productivity management system. Remember, we are concerned with *managerial functions* and not the technical functions (i.e., sales, accounting, design, production) of resource management. In other words, we want to answer the question: What do managers in all technical functions and at all levels do to achieve productivity?

There are two basic dimensions to the managerial task of productivity improvement. Each is practiced by every manager at all levels. Indeed, the application of these principles is even more important at the middle manager and supervisor level because this is the level at which results are achieved. The two dimensions are:

1. *Managing subordinates.* Those actions necessary to make the worker achieve.

2. *Managing work.* Those actions necessary to make work productive.

The System

The System for Managing Productivity is summarized in Figure 2–4. The remainder of this book is devoted to the development of this model. The following topics are discussed in subsequent chapters:

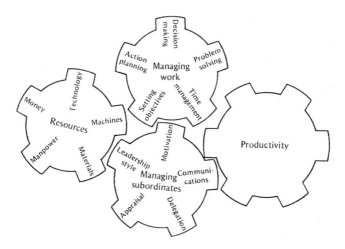

Figure 2–4. A System for Productivity Management

Managing Subordinates: Factors Affecting Productivity

Job Development Matching the job to the subordinate's skills and abilities so that he or she is motivated to perform better.

Appraisal Performance appraisal based on results rather than personality traits or attitudes unrelated to productivity. Utilizing appraisal to set goals, communicate, and provide feedback.

Subordinate Development Providing, through coaching, counseling, and goal setting, the opportunity for the subordinate to grow into more responsible jobs.

Communications Upward communication through formal and informal channels. Basic fundamentals of communicating through results.

Delegation and Control Principles of good delegation without abdication. Results management and self-control.

Leadership Style Requirements of good leadership and motivation. How to resolve the apparent conflict between production and people needs and how to motivate through results management.

Organization Style Breaking through the bureaucratic barrier and getting results through team organization.

Managing Work

Setting Objectives Principles of a "Management by Objectives" program and how objectives are set in the superior–subordinate team.

Problem Solving The rational approach to identification and specification of problem situations.

Decision Making The creative process of identifying alternative courses of action to reach an objective or solve a problem. The analytical approach to weighing and selecting the best alternative.

Action Planning The process of converting a decision, objective, or problem definition into a systematic plan. Setting controls over the plan. Development of an individual productivity program.

Time Management How to organize and plan your individual work time in order to be more effective as a manager.

CHECK YOUR CONCEPTS OF
PRODUCTIVITY MANAGEMENT

	Yes	No
1. Can you describe a job in terms of the components of a system?	( )	( )
Your job?	( )	( )
Your subordinate's job?	( )	( )
2. Can you define a job or its productivity in terms of the ratio between output and input?	( )	( )
Your job?	( )	( )
Your subordinate's job?	( )	( )
3. Can you measure the output of the activity of a job with a yardstick that measures results?	( )	( )
Your job?	( )	( )
Your subordinate's job?	( )	( )
4. Can you describe one or more instances in which organizational integration involving your job is lacking and why?	( )	( )
5. Does your company maintain a classical organization structure?	( )	( )
If yes, can you name the disadvantages?	( )	( )
Can you describe how results management might overcome these disadvantages?	( )	( )
6. Can you describe how productivity can be improved by better management of subordinates?	( )	( )
7. Can you describe how productivity can be improved by better management of work?	( )	( )

3

Managing Subordinates

Motivation and Productivity, Job Development, and Appraisal

Motivation and Productivity
Factors Affecting Productivity
Job Development
Appraisal
Managing Subordinates: Check Your
    Readiness

It is widely agreed that the greatest untapped potential for increasing productivity lies in the motivation and management of people in the work situation. This idea, somewhat slow to catch on, is now being promoted by management and labor alike. At General Motors, the "organization person's organization," many managers believe that recapturing the interest of their workers—or at least getting them to tolerate life on the assembly line—is one of the crucial problems to be solved in the remainder of the century. Most chief executives will freely admit that their most important decisions are about people. Even unions, historically concerned with little more than pay and benefits, are now adopting policies regarding the quality of work life as it relates to motivation and participation. Quoted here is a portion of a recent policy statement by the United Automobile Workers (UAW):

> Achieving job satisfaction includes not only decent working conditions, it must move to a higher plateau where the worker is not merely the adjunct of the tool, but in which he participates in the decision-making process which concerns his welfare on the job. This calls for a departure from the miniaturization and oversimplification of the jobs, symbolic of "scientific management" to a system which embraces broader distribution of authority, increasing rather than diminishing responsibility, combined with the engineering of more interesting jobs, with the opportunity to exercise a meaningful measure of autonomy and to utilize more varied skills. It requires tapping the creative and innovative ingenuity of the worker and his direct participation in the decisions involved in his job.[1]

The modern manager must consider not only what is right for the company but what is right for the individual as well. In the past we have ordinarily considered these two requirements as conflicting. The problem now is to combine them into a single approach that meets the needs of the company as well as its personnel. It can be done.

In this chapter we will examine those factors which affect productivity and relate them to modern motivational philosophy and practice. Throughout I will argue that a *management by results* approach is the central theme and the operational vehicle by which we can achieve productivity. Results management motivates the manager and the subordinate to action because each decides the job necessary to get the results demanded by the work. It is a philosophy of management that rests on the concepts of human action, behavior, and motivation.

---

[1] U.S. House of Representatives, *Hearings on the National Center for Productivity Act of 1975.* Washington, D.C.: U.S. Government Printing Office, 1975, p. 215.

MOTIVATION AND PRODUCTIVITY

Most of the readers of this book have probably been exposed to the basic conceptual aspects of human motivation as it applies to the job situation. The fundamental notion is that when employees are provided an opportunity to utilize their talents and potential, they will perform at a higher level of productivity, make fewer mistakes, and achieve a higher level of personal satisfaction. I will summarize the mainstream of existing theory by presenting a thumbnail sketch of the principles developed by three contemporary experts: Abraham Maslow, Douglas McGregor, and Frederick Herzberg.

Maslow, the father of humanist psychology, concluded that human wants form a hierarchy which runs from lower to higher order needs; from basic physical drives (hunger, thirst, sex) to higher order psychological needs (self-esteem, accomplishment). The highest order need he called *self-actualization*. As one level of the hierarchy is reasonably satisfied, the next level becomes the more potent motivator. His statement that "man lives by bread alone—only when there is no bread" illustrates the point that as the economic wants become increasingly satisfied, it becomes less and less satisfying to obtain more economic rewards. Hence the promise of money or other economic rewards is not a motivator once basic needs are met.

Maslow's theory has two important lessons for the manager. First, within most organizations, sizable numbers of employees move swiftftly to the satisfaction of lower order needs but become frustrated because their opportunities for self-actualization (growth and development) are thwarted and full utilization of their talents is blocked. They must either be satisfied with something less than optimum job satisfaction or find outside involvement to fulfill their needs for meaningful accomplishment. The second lesson to be learned from Maslow is that money is not the motivator we thought it was. This may be hard to accept but a moment's reflection may convince you that although a person may work harder because of the promise of money, he or she is not motivated. There is a substantial difference. The problem with money is that the worker must constantly be re-cycled by some form of behavior reinforcement with either the carrot or the stick. Neither case illustrates motivation. The worker "moves" but isn't motivated. Only self-actualization related to the job will achieve that.

A second highly popular theory of motivation and human behavior has been advanced by Douglas McGregor: the concept of the Theory X and the Theory Y managerial styles. The classical approach to management is represented by Theory X, which maintains that there is no satisfaction in the work itself, that humans avoid work as much as possible, that positive direction and tight control over workers is necessary, and that workers possess little ambition or enthusiasm for their work. The human relations approach of Theory Y, the antithesis of Theory X, states that workers exercise self-direction and seek responsibility if properly motivated. Theory Y is a *participative* approach. We will talk more about this topic when we examine leadership styles.

It remained for Frederick Herzberg to show how managers can move toward adopting Theory Y assumptions while satisfying the higher order needs of self-actualization for their subordinates. He pointed out that when economic rewards and other lower-level needs are met, they are diminished in importance as positive incentives, but their capacity to create dissatisfaction rapidly increases if they are not satisfied. He said that economic rewards cease to be "incentives" and become "hygiene factors." If not properly taken care of—that is, if there is dissatisfaction with the economic rewards—they become deterrents. On the positive side, Herzberg found that another group of factors, the *motivators*, tended to produce job satisfaction and productivity. These motivators center around the job itself or the job content and included *achievement, growth, participation,* and *responsibility.*

Herzberg's role in motivational theory cannot be denied. He has re-focused management's attention from the classical Theory X assumptions and hygiene factors (e.g., pay, benefits, environmental conditions) to the far more important motivator factors of achievement: recognition, and the work itself. These factors are the ones that hold promise for increased productivity and job satisfaction. Too often in the past, management's motivational attempts have been limited to the hygiene areas.

It is important to understand the difference between hygiene and motivational factors surrounding the subordinate's job. To illustrate these differences, Table 3–1 contains a list of potential assignments for a staff secretary. These have been identified as motivator (M) or hygiene (H).

What does all this mean in terms of our *system for managing productivity?* It means that first we must identify those job factors that motivate and hence affect the productivity of subordinates. It means that second we must operationalize these factors. In other words, we combine theory and practice in order to achieve results through managing subordinates.

FACTORS AFFECTING PRODUCTIVITY

Few topics have been as discussed, debated, researched, and written about as the behavioral science implications of productivity and job satisfaction.

Table 3–1. Hygiene and Motivational Factors Surrounding Job of Staff Secretary

Job Assignment	Motivator	Hygiene
Go to lunch with boss		X
Set objectives for office routine	X	
Select incoming letter for self reply	X	
Provide advice to department on policy	X	
Set own working hours		X
Have own office		X
Present recommendations at meetings	X	
Attend departmental meetings		X
Eliminate coffee making duties	X	X
Get new typewriter		X
Farm out xerox work	X	X
Get salary increase		X
Prepare expense accounts		X
Approve expense accounts	X	
Change title to staff coordinator		X
Attend convention	X	X

The most important question in the field of management remains: *How do I motivate employees?*

Research and observation tell us that there are nine important factors (motivators) that need to be taken into account if an organization is to effect the changes that are necessary to increase productivity and profitability. These are summarized here:

1. *Work* that is challenging, creative, and interesting and provides an opportunity for "stretch" performance.

2. *Participation* in decisions that have a direct effect on the individual's job.

3. *Compensation* that is tied to performance and to sharing in productivity gains. This requires realistic *appraisal.*

4. *Communication and authority* channels that are simplified.

5. *Supervision* that is competent.

6. *Recognition* of achievement.

7. *Self-development* opportunity.

8. Opportunity for *stewardship*, care of and attention to customer and co-worker needs.

9. *Organizational styles* and patterns that are more flexible.

   Providing for these job satisfaction and motivational needs is not a simple task. Indeed, it is very complex. No simplistic change or group of changes, such as revised pay schedules or job enrichment, alone will suffice, nor will any misdirected notions of "human relations" or paternalism.

   We do know that certain basic techniques, methods, and programs are available to the organization and to the individual manager that, taken together, can go a long way toward creating the proper climate for productivity. We will call these *Results Management Methods* and they form the basis of our system of managing subordinates. They are:

1. *Job Development.* Matching the content and level of an employee's job responsibility to his or her skills and abilities.

2. *Performance Appraisal.* The process of appraising a subordinate's performance against previously established goals. This provides feedback on performance, a tool for self-development, and a device for recognition for performance.

3. *Subordinate Development.* Providing the environment for continuous learning, self-development, and growth on the job.

4. *Communication.* Improving the communication process using upward communication so that subordinates are informed about matters which affect their jobs.

5. *Leadership Style.* The adoption of leadership and supervisory styles that promote "results thinking" and hence productivity and job satisfaction.

6. *Delegation and Control.* Learning and practicing the art of delegation utilizing self-control by subordinates.

7. *Organizational Style.* Adopting an organizational form that provides for flexibility in authority and communication and overcomes the inflexibility of the classical bureaucracy.

   The matrix shown in Figure 3–1 indicates how our factors affecting productivity can be achieved by using the seven results management methods listed above.

   The remainder of this chapter and chapter 4 will discuss in more detail the principles behind these methods and how we can achieve greater productivity. These seven methods provide the central core of our system for managing subordinates.

MANAGEMENT METHODS

FACTORS AFFECTING PRODUCTIVITY	Job development	Appraisal	Subordinate development	Communications	Delegation and control	Leadership style	Organization style
Work that is challenging, creative, and interesting	X	X	X		X		X
Participation in decisions affecting the job	X	X	X	X	X	X	X
Compensation tied to performance	X	X	X	X			
Simplification of channels of communication			X	X	X	X	X
Competent supervisor	X	X	X	X	X	X	
Recognition for achievement	X	X	X	X	X	X	X
Opportunity for self development	X	X	X	X	X	X	X
Opportunity for stewardship	X	X	X	X	X		X
Organization style that is flexible			X	X	X	X	X

Figure 3-1. Management Methods and Factors Affecting Productivity Note: X indicates the management method that can be effective in implementing the factor affecting productivity.

JOB DEVELOPMENT[2]

The story goes that job development or job enlargement was discovered at IBM when the company's founder, Thomas J. Watson, Sr., saw a woman operator sitting idly at her machine. When asked why she was not working, the woman replied: "I have to sit and wait for the setup man to change the tool setting for a new run." Watson asked: "Couldn't you change the tool setting yourself?" The woman replied: "Of course I could but I am not allowed to." Upon further examination Watson learned that in addition to waiting for setup men, additional idle time was spent wait-

[2] The term *job development* is similar to but more comprehensive than the popular terms *job enlargement* or *job enrichment*. It is unfortunate that the latter two terms have become associated with gimmickry such as horizontal loading of jobs, focus on salary aspects, and failure to deliver on motivational promises. Job development, on the other hand, focuses on all three areas of worker utilization: the job, the employee, and the team or work group of which the employee is a part. *See* William N. Penzer, *Productivity and Motivation Through Job Engineering.* New York: AMACOM, 1973.

ing for inspectors to inspect the finished products of the same workers. Watson reasoned, correctly, that little time would be required to train the workers to perform both additional tasks of setting up the machine and inspecting the finished product. He instituted these changes and the resulting job development and elimination of excess task specialization resulted in better quality, fewer losses due to scrap, and a steady increase in productivity. Moreover, workers reported greater job satisfaction and more interest in their work. This philosophy has pervaded IBM since that time.

There is little doubt that millions of employees at all levels of organizations are underutilized and misutilized in the United States today. This waste of human resources can result in serious consequences for company productivity. In the personnel management area it can account for turnover, tardiness, accidents, high rates of grievances, strikes, and even outright sabotage. In the product and service areas these consequences can range from low product quality to disinterest in or even antagonism toward customer requirements.

Two actions can go a long way toward improving productivity through better personnel utilization: (1) match the job with the person; and (2) remove the boredom from the job.

Matching the job with the person involves developing or engineering the job so that the job responsibilities, content, and level match the employee's skills and abilities. It is worth noting the difference between *content* and *level* of the match. If a job calls for a level of responsibility that is lower than the person's ability, it is not a good match even though the job content and employee overlap. A good job–employee match includes a reasonable overlap between skill and job demands and a level of responsibility that provides room for growth and development of the individual.

Removing the boredom from the job is becoming an increasing challenge. Popular expressions like "blue collar blues" and "white collar monotony" are becoming commonplace but these trite phrases mislead people into thinking that job monotony, boredom, and dissatisfaction are confined to the assembly line or the clerical level. This is not the case. In many organizations dissatisfaction occurs at all levels from the floor sweeper to the executive suite.

The manager who wants to improve the job–employee match or to remove some of the boredom from work is faced with two contradictory arguments. On the one hand, traditional "scientific management" and the industrial engineer calls for the programming and standardization of specialized tasks using the techniques of work simplification, methods design, process and activity charts and so on. On the other hand the emerging approach of the behavioral scientists tell us that task specialization is bad and we should engineer the job so that employees want to channel their interests toward their work.

The two approaches have tended to exaggerate their differences rather than similarities and a natural schism has developed. The route to overcoming the apparent contradiction between "scientific management" and "behavioral science" lies in a marriage of the two. The industrial engineer must recognize that the traditional view of the worker as a "hand"[3] must be changed because the whole person comes with it. The *integrated* approach is one that is based on job development. These three approaches to job design: (1) industrial engineering; (2) behavioral science; and (3) integrated, are shown in Table 3–2.

Three Principles of Job Development

There are three fundamental principles of job development:

1. Vertical loading

2. Closure

3. Feedback on performance

1. *Vertical loading* refers to the job–employee match previously described wherein the employee's job responsibility and decision-making participation is enlarged to meet the individual's skills, abilities, and potential. This is in contrast to the "ratchet principle" or traditional *horizontal* loading that merely increases the volume of work that an employee does at a particular level of difficulty. For example, the restaurant busboy who is assigned the additional duties of sweeping up the floor is experiencing horizontal loading without additional responsibility or discretion. However, if he is given responsibility for inventory control of dishes and tableware he is experiencing vertical job loading. It becomes immediately apparent that *the delegation of the manager's own duties is the best way to enlarge the job of subordinates.*

The job development and vertical job loading approach is demonstrated in Figure 3–1, page 29. Those job assignments identified as motivators involve the vertical job loading of the staff secretary.

2. *Closure* is the characteristic of a job that provides the employees with a sense of contribution to the organization and an identification with the end product of their work. The typical assembly line job fails to provide closure because the workers perform miniscule, repetitive parts of the whole job and begin to get the feeling that they are "nameless, faceless cogs in the big machine."

---

[3] In high technology industries a technical worker, such as a design engineer, is sometimes referred to as a "head."

Table 3–2. Comparison of Three Different Approaches to Job Design

Scientific Management	Behavioral Science	Integrated
Specialization of tasks	Provide task variety to avoid boredom	To the extent that long-term time or cost variables are not substantially increased, employees should:
Minimize number of operations one employee performs	Enlarge the job to meet the skills and ability of the worker	Be allowed to monitor their own workpace
Eliminate unnecessary motions and operations	Provide feedback on performance	Determine which methods are best for accomplishing a particular task
No idle or waiting time	Provide job closure or job identification	Be assigned primary responsibility for quality
Let the worker work and the supervisor plan and control	Self control of significant aspects of the work	Be encouraged to be the true job experts
	Participation in problem solving, planning, and controlling	Be encouraged to become involved in decision making regarding unit problems and solutions
	Opportunity to learn new skills	Be provided opportunity for more responsible, challenging, and self fulfilling work assignments

In the case of the busboy above, closure could be provided to his job if he were assigned the responsibility for purchase of supplies.

3. *Feedback on performance* is a necessary part of job development and it makes good supervisory sense. Too frequently superiors depend upon variance reports or annual performance appraisals to provide feedback. These formal devices are not only too infrequent but in almost every case are too late to provide the type of "real time" feedback required.

The notion of real time feedback can be understood by using an analogy of a bowler. He rolls the ball and gets immediate feedback on the number of pins he has knocked down. Now imagine that a curtain is thrown up immediately after the ball is rolled so that the bowler is unable to see how many pins he has knocked down. Somewhat in the manner of an employee he shouts: "How did I do?" and somewhat in the manner of the manager, someone shouts from behind the curtain: "Don't worry, I will let you know [by variance report] next week." Obviously no one would want to bowl under these circumstances because no feedback on performance is available.

The message here is that the supervisor should provide this feedback or, better still, build it into the job. Feedback is also a necessary ingredient of self-development, coaching, and counseling.

To return to our system of productivity management, we can see how the focus on results approach is important for the implementation of job development. The connection is summarized in Table 3–3.

Table 3–3.

Job Development Principle	Focus on Results
Match the job to the employee	Results expected from the job provide yardstick of evaluation.
Remove boredom from job	Integrated approach to job engineering requires definition of output in terms of results.
Vertical job loading	Enlarged responsibility defined in terms of results expected.
Closure	Job results provides sense of employee identification with the job.
Feedback on performance	Feedback is best provided in terms of performance against predetermined goal.

APPRAISAL

Any manager with "hands on" experience with performance appraisal almost invariably finds the job distasteful. Research has shown that in those companies without a formal control system over the process, fewer than half of the appraisals are ever completed. In my own experience with hundreds of supervisors and middle managers I have found that the appraisal process and communication are the two most frequently mentioned problems. They don't like either role, whether it be the "appraisor" or the "appraisee." The process inhibits more often than it promotes communication.

In general, there are three reasons for supervisory resistance to the appraisal process: (1) Supervisors don't like to criticize a subordinate and have to handle the inevitable argument that follows; (2) they feel that they are not equipped to properly perform the appraisal of a subordinate or to handle the accompanying interview; and (3) they have a general mistrust of the techniques and procedures surrounding the appraisal process.

The subordinates usually dislike the process also. Unless they are one of the few selected for high praise, the employees almost always feel that their performance has been judged unfairly.

The general failure of the appraisal system to operate as expected is unfortunate. Properly used, the performance appraisal can become a fine tool for improved motivation, communication, self-development, and hence productivity.

The Problems With Performance Appraisal

Most organizations with appraisal programs have two things in common. They follow the textbook definition and consider the appraisal process as a formal evaluation of employee actions over a previous time period. Secondly, virtually all have some performance appraisal form. The similarity among companies ends there.

Deficiencies in practice can be summarized under the five broad areas discussed below.

1. Focusing on the *reward/punishment* aspect tends to detract from the real purpose of an appraisal session. When viewed this way, the interview frequently turns into either a whitewash job or a faultfinding session. If the former, the employee may go away with false hopes for promotion or pay increases or a false sense of job security. Faultfinding appraisals

frequently regress into personality clashes resulting from statements about behavior and performance that have not been previously communicated. In any case, both the boss and the subordinate frequently depart with feelings of distress or ill-will.

2. Appraisals based on *personality traits* (e.g., loyalty, initiative, cooperation, attitude, and so on) are bad news. They obscure the real purpose of appraisal which is focus on results. In practically no case is the subordinate motivated to better productivity. (More on this later.)

3. *Emphasis on the system* is an all too frequent complaint. When it is viewed as a mandatory technique or procedure, or something the Personnel Department "dreamed up," the system becomes the ends and not the means. Reflect upon our definition of the input managers in chapter 2; they emphasized form and administration (doing things right) as opposed to process and management (doing the right things).

4. There is a general *confusion about the objectives* of performance review. Rarely is improved productivity a stated objective of appraisal nor is it viewed as a vehicle to focus on results. Instead, its purpose is frequently seen as a catch-all of procedures related to general personnel administration: wage and salary review, placement, development, and advancement. When this approach occurs, both employee and manager become confused and adopt defensive behavior regarding the process.

5. *Nonproductive behavior* is a frequent result of appraisal. Although the process implies precision, in reality it is quite imprecise (unless based on results) and filled with personal judgment and emotion. There is a tendency to do something *to* the employees, not *with* them. The appraisal becomes, at best, a hygenic aspect of motivation, at worst, an emotional letdown for both superior and subordinate.

The Job Description Problem

Some of the difficulty surrounding the focus on activities can be traced to a great American industrial institution—the job description. Often these are written in terms of activities and general statements of responsibilities rather than in terms of what is expected from the job. An examination of Figure 3–2, a typical job description for a production foreman, will reveal that careful adherence to the language of the description tends to turn the employee's effort away from the real output of the subsystem.

A solution to this difficulty lies in including a statement of expected results in the job description. Aside from all the other advantages we have mentioned, such action would provide a basis for appraisal.

Job Description: Foreman, Line #1

General

The foreman of line number one is responsible for the manufacture of
assigned products in accordance with the applicable production
schedule. He or she is also responsible for cost budgets and quality
specifications as well as liaison with other departments considered
necessary to insure uninterrupted production. He or she will perform
these duties in accordance with company policies, procedures, and
instructions.

Specific Duties

1. Schedule tools for production line setup.
2. Schedule raw materials and manpower for production schedule.
    This applies to tools and maintenance also.
3. Take appropriate action to minimize absenteeism.
4. Maintain discipline for employees on the shift.
5. Maintain liaison with shipping to insure adequate finished
    goods shipments.
6. Communicate company policies, procedures, and other
    information as required.
7. Provide information to Personnel Department and Cost Accounting
    as required.
8. Comply with provisions of union contract.
9. Minimize downtime due to machine failure.
10. Take other action as required or as directed by company
    management.

Working Hours

First shift: 7:30 a.m. to 4:00 p.m. Monday to Friday
Second shift: 3:30 p.m. to 12:00 a.m. Monday to Friday

Immediate Supervisor

Plant Production Superintendent

Figure 3–2.

The Problem of Personality and Trait Appraisal

Regardless of how an organization views the purposes and needs of its
appraisal program, many of them base all or a part of their employee
evaluation on how the supervisor perceives the subordinate's behavior,
attitudes, personality, and job knowledge. This *traitist* approach is designed to let the employee know where he or she "stands" with the boss.
This widespread approach is illustrated in Figure 3–3 which is a typical
company appraisal form. Many managers express real misgivings about a

_____Corporation   Employee Appraisal Form

Name_____ Employee #_____ Date_____

Using the code below rate the employee on each of the factors listed
with the code that most closely indicates his or her performance in
comparison with the requirements of the job.

1. Outstanding. The best possible for the job. 2. Very Good.
Beyond the requirements for good performance. 3. Good. Meets the
requirements for the job. This is the basic standard. 4. Fair.
Performance is barely satisfactory and needs improvement in basic
aspects of job. 5. Unsatisfactory. Deficient.

Job Factor	Explanation	Rating
Judgment	Are his or her decisions based on sound reasoning?	( )
Human Relations	Does he or she cooperate with and effectively influence people?	( )
Attitude	Does he or she show interest and enthusiasm and a desire to improve performance?	( )
Quantity of Work	Does he or she produce an acceptable quantity?	( )
Quality of Work	Is his or her work accurate, thorough, and acceptable?	( )
Communications	Is he or she effective in written and oral expression?	( )
Initiative	Is he or she a self starter, seeking out opportunities and responsibility?	( )
Leadership	Does he or she motivate fellow workers and subordinates?	( )
Cost Conscious	Is he or she interested in better performance at lower cost?	( )
Integrity	Is he or she reliable, trustworthy and honest?	( )
Personal	Neatness, character, etc.	( )

What is the major positive aspects of the employee's work?

State the major area in which the employee should improve.

Figure 3-3. Typical Appraisal Form   37

system based on personality traits and are uncomfortable when put in the position of "playing God" or "playing psychiatrist."

Based on our discussion of productivity and motivation thus far it is easy to summarize those reasons why the traitist approach to appraisal should be abandoned as the only device for employee evaluation:

1. It is resisted by superior and subordinate alike.

2. It doesn't measure performance in terms of results.

3. It focuses on activities rather than output.

4. Appraisal based on traits is not a motivator.

5. There is no proven correlation between traits and productivity.

6. Many managers are not qualified to "play psychiatrist."

Summary: Appraisal Based on Results

A *results management* approach to appraisal will help to overcome the several shortcomings of the traditional traitist system. It will also help to achieve the real objectives of appraisal: (1) improvement of productivity and results; (2) the development of people for both organizational and individual needs; and (3) improvement of the superior–subordinate relationship.

The results approach calls for the subordinate to determine personal performance goals in terms of expected results. At the end of the appraisal period, or as often as necessary, the subordinate makes a personal appraisal. This in turn provides the vehicle by which superior and subordinate jointly determine the nature of the job, the results expected, and the performance of the individual.

This approach will also significantly improve the process of communication. An appraisal based on what a person has done well and what can be done in the future, a discussion surrounding the individual's direction for self-development, provides basic foundations for communication. Taken in this light, appraisal is not a task to be resisted but an opportunity to jointly establish a future direction.

The shortcomings of traditional appraisal and a summary of how results management can help overcome them are shown in Table 3–4.

The organization that adopts an appraisal system based on results rather than personality traits is on the right road to productivity improvement. A companion system would include job descriptions that are written in terms of results expected rather than vague responsibilities relating to activities.

Table 3–4.

Shortcomings of Traditional Appraisal	How Results Management Can Help
Focus on reward/punishment for past performance	Focus on results for future
Emphasis on the system	Emphasis on productivity
Uncertain objectives	Objectives stated in terms of results
Nonproductive behavior	Motivation for achievement
Trait appraisal	Appraisal based on goals
Vague job descriptions	Superior–subordinate joint determination of job requirements

MANAGING SUBORDINATES: CHECK YOUR READINESS

	Yes	No
1. Have you identified the motivational factors in your subordinate's job assignment that produce productivity?	( )	( )

If no, review the motivational theories of Maslow, McGregor, and Herzberg.

	Yes	No
2. Does the job assignment of your subordinates match the person?	( )	( )

If no, mix the scientific management approach with the behavioral approach per Table 3–2.

3. Do your subordinates complain:

	Yes	No
The job is boring?	( )	( )
They can't see the results of their job and how it fits into the big picture?	( )	( )
They aren't getting feedback on the performance in their job?	( )	( )

If yes, practice the techniques of job development based on results.

4. Does your performance appraisal system:

	Yes	No
Emphasize traits and personality?	( )	( )
Focus on rewards and punishment?	( )	( )
Emphasize the system and not results?	( )	( )
Produce nonproductive behavior?	( )	( )

If yes, write job descriptions and performance appraisals based on results.

4

Managing Subordinates

Development and Communication

Developing Subordinates
Communication
Checklist for Subordinate Development and
     Communication

It is widely accepted among managers and workers alike that the attitudes and motivation, and hence the productivity, of employees are affected by self-development opportunities and improved communication. People want the chance to grow, to have an opportunity to undertake increased responsibility, and to achieve recognition for their performance.

Communication, the second topic of this chapter, is near the top of everyone's list of things to do to improve any organization's productivity. Most supervisors will agree that simplified channels of communication and authority would make their job more productive and help their subordinates achieve more.

DEVELOPING SUBORDINATES

An essential requirement for achievement in an individual's work is a continuous learning process. This learning process is not only an effective motivator for improved performance (and, incidentally, self-satisfaction), but it fulfills the need that most of us have to keep abreast of new knowledge and avoid obsolescence. A side benefit is that workers who are engaged in learning will be much less resistant to change. Indeed, the chances are good that they will recommend innovation and change.

It is the job of every supervisor to provide the environment for and encourage self-development by subordinates. We have already seen how coaching and counseling during the appraisal process is one means to provide this encouragement. Another is formal training. But in terms of our system of productivity management, two additional principles of subordinate development should be remembered:

1. The motivation of a "stretch" objective.

2. The Pygmalion Effect or the self-fulfilling prophecy.

Setting a "Stretch" Objective

Procter & Gamble has long been recognized as a citadel of excellent management and financial success. The chief executive says: "We don't believe in mothering our managers. We like to give people responsibility very quickly, and that means putting them in jobs they aren't quite ready for." The results of such a philosophy of development was summarized by one middle-level manager: "You believe you can succeed because you know the company thinks you can. Each successive assignment, which at first seems like a crisis, reinforces that feeling."

This Procter & Gamble philosophy of a "reach out" goal is to be admired but it reflects a curious dilemma for the managers. On the one hand they know that their subordinates will not be motivated to reach high levels of performance unless they consider the boss's high expectations realistic and achievable. On the other hand, goals that are easy to achieve and do not represent any challenge are not only nonproductive but fail also in the other motivational aspects of the job. The trick is to maintain in the subordinate a state of *mild stress* by mutually setting goals that make him or her "stretch" to achieve them.

My golf handicap is eighteen. This means that on the average my score is ninety-six. Now if my goal were to reduce my average score to ninety-five I would not be motivated because the target is too easy; it doesn't make me "stretch." On the other hand, if I were required to shoot an average score of say, eighty, I would simply stop playing the game of golf. Instead of "stretching," I would be in shock! The goal is clearly beyond reach.

Research has shown that targets that are set too high generally result in negative attitudes and a drop in performance by employees. The old "carrot and stick" philosophy, the practice of dangling the carrot just beyond the donkey's reach, is not good motivational practice.

The relationship between motivation to succeed and expectation of success can be represented by the curve shown in Figure 4–1. The degree of motivation and effort will rise until the probability of reaching the goal reaches approximately fifty percent, then begins to fall even though the expectation of success continues on a lessened basis. Thus the employee can be expected to have little or no motivation to succeed when the goal is perceived as being practically certain or practically impossible to attain.

The message is clear. The results expected (not the activity) of sub-

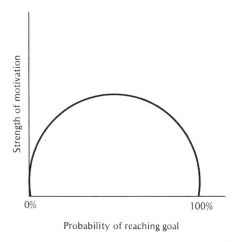

Probability of reaching goal

Figure 4–1.   Relationship Between Motivation to Succeed and Probability of Goal Success

ordinates should be mutually agreed upon at a level that keeps them under mild stress for their attainment; a "stretch" objective. It follows naturally that since the expectation of success is substantially less than one hundred percent, reasonable failure to meet the target is not cause for recrimination or punishment. Progress should be measured periodically through feedback and the target adjusted as required to maintain mild stress but not shock.

The Pygmalion Effect: A Self-fulfilling Prophecy

In Greek mythology, Pygmalion was a sculptor who carved an ivory statue of the ideal woman. Because his creation was so beautiful and life-like he fell in love with the statue and his steadfast belief led Venus to bring the statue to life. Later, this Greek myth was to inspire George Bernard Shaw's play, *Pygmalion,* which in turn formed the basis for the musical hit, *"My Fair Lady."* In this play Professor Higgins took Liza Doolittle, a London flower girl, and turned her into a charming lady. You may recall Liza's dialogue:

> ". . . The difference between a lady and a flower girl is not how she behaves, but how she's treated. I shall always be a flower girl to Professor Higgins, because he always treats me as a flower girl and always will, but I know I can be a lady to you, because you always treat me as a lady and always will."

Many managers, like Professor Higgins, unintentionally treat their subordinates in a way that leads to lower performance than they could normally achieve. This reflects the well-known principle that one person's expectations can influence the behavior of another. This concept—known as the Pygmalion Effect or the Self-fulfilling Prophecy—states that when one predicts an event, the expectation of the event changes the behavior of the "prophet" in such a way as to make the event more likely to happen.

The notion that one person's behavior is influenced by another person's expectations has been recognized for a long time by physicians and behavioral scientists but only recently by managers. Among physicians it is known as the "placebo effect." A placebo is a harmless preparation given merely to humor the patient but if the patient believes it will help, it will.[1]

---

[1] An opposite effect is also possible. Numerous people are afflicted with iatrogenic (physician *caused*) illnesses. This occurs when the doctor is approached by someone complaining of a few symptoms. The doctor classifies these symptoms, gives them a name, and obligingly tells the patient he is sick. From that day on the patient becomes sick.

A Harvard University behavioral scientist, Dr. Robert Rosenthal, coined the term "Pygmalion Effect" and conducted a number of experiments to test his hypothesis. One of these involved the behavior of rats in solving the problems of a maze. He randomly chose two groups of rats and arbitrarily labeled them "maze bright" and "maze dull." Unaware of the random choice and arbitrary designation, student researchers adopted the conclusion that the rats were, indeed, "maze bright" and "maze dull" despite the fact that the rats were randomly chosen. The researchers even found the "maze bright" rats to be more pleasant to handle and more cooperative.

Another Rosenthal experiment tested the Pygmalion Effect in an elementary school. He randomly chose children from eighteen classrooms and labeled them "intellectual bloomers." Teachers were told that these children could be expected to show remarkable gains during the year. In actuality, the difference between the "intellectual bloomers" and the remainder of the children was solely in the minds of the teachers. Eight months later the "intellectual bloomers" showed an overall IQ gain of four points over the "normal" children. More remarkable were the attitudes of the teachers. They thought the brighter students were appealing, more affectionate, and better adjusted. The conclusion: the higher performing and better liked students had superior performance because it was what had been expected of them.

There is an important message here for managers. In the language of psychologist Rensis Likert, "If a high level of performance is to be achieved, it appears to be necessary for a supervisor to have high performance goals and a contagious enthusiasm as to the importance of these goals." Two examples will illustrate this: "Sweeney's Miracle" and the high aptitude welders.

Professor James Sweeney of Tulane University believed that he could teach a poorly-educated person to be a good computer operator. For a demonstration of his theory he chose George Johnson, a black, uneducated janitor. Johnson was doing very well under Sweeney's tutelage until the Personnel Department decided that computer operators must have a certain IQ score. Johnson's IQ indicated that he couldn't learn to type, much less operate and program a computer. But Sweeney insisted, even under the threat of resignation, that Johnson should be allowed to continue his training.

At last report Professor Sweeney is directing the computer center and George Johnson is in charge of the main computer room and is responsible for training new computer operators. Johnson succeeded because of Sweeney's expectations and what Sweeney believed about his own teaching ability.

In a Texas experiment, five welding trainees were selected at random and their supervisors were told that they had an exceptionally high aptitude for welding, despite the fact that they were no better or worse than the average. At the end of the six month course, the supervisors rated these "high aptitude" trainees significantly higher than the others. Remarkably, so did their peers. The group also performed significantly higher on a standard welding test and on a written examination. By all measures they outperformed the control group. Why? Because of expectations of themselves and their supervisors. Their performance was a self-fulfilling prophecy.

Unfortunately, the reverse is also true. Negative expectations usually result in negative performance. Thus we have negative self-fulfilling prophecies. Indeed, these are more prevalent and far more damaging to productivity than positive expectations. The only way to break the cycle of negative self-fulfilling prophecies is to change the concept of work and superior–subordinate relationships. We must think positive!

If we assume, as we must, that the best managers are those that increase the motivation and productivity of their subordinates, then it follows that these managers should be "positive Pygmalions." They should expect more and communicate these expectations. They should try and develop these characteristics:

1. Believe in themselves and have confidence in what they are doing. This confidence will be transmitted to subordinates.

2. Have faith in their ability to develop their subordinates; to select, train, and motivate them. Subordinates will justify this faith because it is what is expected of them.

3. An ability to develop "stretch" goals and communicate this expectation.

4. Develop a preference for reward through achievement of the work group. If *group* rather than *self*-achievement is the higher form of reward, the group will have higher achievement expectations.

In summary, results management will shape the expectations and hence the productivity of subordinates. By communicating the expectations, the supervisor will be a positive influence on attitudes, self-confidence, and self-development.

COMMUNICATION

Communication is second only to motivation as a concern of practicing managers, academicians, and researchers alike. Few topics have been the subject of more research and debate. But the question still remains: "How do I communicate?" The more we seem to talk about it, the less we seem to experience.

There is no doubt that productivity is directly affected by the way we communicate in organizations. A breakdown in communications is just as costly as the breakdown of machines, the loss of sales, a poor engineering design, or material stockouts. Indeed, the operation of all other subsystems of the business and the integration between subsystems depends on good communication. If we can draw an analogy between the company and the human body, organization structure is the anatomy and communication is the nervous system. Both are required to make the system work.

The process is at once simple and complicated. It revolves around three basic factors: a sender, a receiver, and a message. The sender and the receiver can be either individuals or groups since the process works irrespective of the numbers involved. The word communication is derived from the Latin "communis," meaning commonness, and it is this commonness of meaning in the message that the sender and receiver are trying to achieve through the communication process. Commonness in meaning is difficult to achieve.

Downward Communication

The communication cycle is not complete until the sender receives some sort of feedback regarding the receipt of the message by the receiver. The sender must evaluate the impact of the message by some action or response that is appropriate to the message and the receiver. A lack of feedback appears to be the central problem throughout history; communication has almost invariably been *downward*. This cannot work.

Downward communication focuses on what we, the senders, want to say and makes the assumption that the sender, i.e., the manager, communicates. But in the overwhelming percentage of instances all the sender does is send. The sender cannot communicate downward anything connected with understanding, especially motivation to productivity. Communication is an act of a receiver and requires communication upward as well, from those who perceive to those who need feedback and understanding that a message has been sent and received. This does not take place when communication is one way.

Formal Communication

Managers today must resolve a curious dilemma. On the one hand they are faced with an information explosion and on the other hand with an increasing number of complex, formal channels to handle the information. One major oil company identified 130 formal channels of organizational communication which included staff meetings, employee forums, employee letters, manuals, bulletin boards, management notices, employee counseling, committee reports, recreation associations, informal talks, and a variety of information systems and reports. Anyone with experience in government or a corporate bureaucracy understands this dilemma. The larger an organization becomes, the more complex are its lines of communication and there is always the danger that techniques and reports can become so institutionalized and inflexible that they take on an existence of their own. The system becomes the end, not the means. It becomes a classic case of thinking in terms of activities and not results.

Some managers believe that information means communication. Nothing is further from the truth. In order for information to communicate, it needs prior agreement on meaning and application, something that few reports and information systems achieve. Indeed, the more information, the greater is the communication gap likely to be. The chief executive of a major high-technology aerospace firm recently eliminated the company's centralized computer-based management information system (CBMIS). He said that the people doing the work at the grass-roots level weren't really using the system, and those who did were swamped with control reports that had become almost meaningless.

Organizations, by their very nature, tend to construct barriers to communication. Information systems, organization structures, authority arrangements, policies, controls, and the other "trappings" of formal organizational complexity make communication difficult, not easy. The challenge is to communicate despite this complexity.

Informal Communication

Communication, of course, is not all formal. The average supervisor concerned with a limited work group is equally concerned with the informal aspects because it is the superior–subordinate and face-to-face oral communications that usually get the job done. This is the way to overcome the formal organizational "trappings."

We communicate in both verbal and nonverbal ways. Our eye contact, physical touch, tone of voice, body posture, facial expressions, and even silence can convey real messages to subordinates. These nonverbal messages can hinder as well as help. Most of us have experienced the "silent treatment" from a cold and uncommunicative boss. This sign of displeasure is frequently more effective than a verbal or written reprimand.

Eye contact is a particularly important conveyor of nonverbal communication. It can communicate concern or lack of it to the observer. In the experiment of the welding trainees described in this chapter, the high achieving welders were shown two photographs of their supervisor. They were exactly alike except that in one photograph the pupils of the eyes had been touched up and enlarged. All of the trainees identified as high achievers felt that the photo with the enlarged eyes looked most like their supervisor. Five of the seven trainees identified as low achievers chose the untouched photographs. Could the pupil of the supervisor's eye communicate a message to the subordinates? Evidently they could.

The spoken word alone has no meaning and cannot communicate. It is merely a part of the total picture. The "silent language," that is, gestures, tone of voice, plus the cultural and social refinements, cannot be distinguished from the spoken language. This phenomenon has been evident among the immigrants to the United States. Handicapped by difficulties of language and culture, most of them learned to communicate with gestures. One appropriate gesture can convey more than a hundred words.

Fundamentals of Communication

Peter Drucker,[2] today's most popular management writer, provides us with an excellent insight into managerial communications. He identified four fundamentals:

1. Communication is perception.

2. Communication is expectation.

3. Communication makes demands.

4. Communication and information are different; largely opposite, yet interdependent.

Perception

Most of us have played fall guy to a small child's inquisitiveness with a question like: "Daddy, is there a sound in the forest if a tree crashes down but there's nobody around to hear it?" If we attempt to answer the question by using logic we do not communicate because the child's perception is quite different from our own. So we say: "No, there is no sound. There are sound waves but there is no sound unless someone hears it . . . perceives it."

This answer, incidentally, is quite correct and illustrates a vital point: it is the recipient who communicates, not the communicator. The com-

---

[2] Peter F. Drucker, *Management: Tasks, Responsibilities, Practices.* New York: Harper & Row Publishers, 1974.

municator only sends a message but there is no communication until the "percipient" perceives it, until the recipient receives it.

Many teachers, public speakers, media "communicators" and managers overlook this fundamental principle; a recipient receives only that which is in terms of his or her own experience. Only those messages which are within a person's cultural and emotional "range of perception" can be understood. Yet we, the managers (communicators), continue to send messages in terms of our own limited experience. What we see so vividly, our subordinates do not see at all; what we argue so logically (we think) has little pertinence to the concerns of our subordinates. "Management" attempts to use logical arguments as to why the union should accept an agreement but "labor" perceives these arguments altogether differently. Consequently there is no communication and the result is impasse and confrontation.

Remember the old story of the three blind men and the elephant? Each man, encountering this strange beast, feels one of the elephant's parts, his leg, his trunk, his hide, and each reaches an unshakeable conclusion regarding what he has felt. What is the message here? The message is that you cannot communicate with the three blind men until you go over and feel the leg, the trunk, and the hide of the elephant. Then you can communicate but only in terms of what the recipient, the true communicator, perceives and why.

Expectation

It is frequently said that beauty is in the eye of the beholder. This cliché means that we perceive what we expect to perceive. We see largely what we expect to see, and we hear largely what we expect to hear. We don't like to be surprised with a message that doesn't fit into our expectations.

Earlier in this chapter we examined the Pygmalion Effect (the self-fulfilling prophecy) and concluded that subordinates tend to behave in accordance with their perception of the superior's expectations.

The principles of expectation and the self-fulfilling prophecies combine to provide us with two useful lessons. First, our expectations have an impact on subordinates and theirs on us. We should convert this into an opportunity to provide a positive influence and communication channel. Second, we should realize that before we can communicate we must know what the subordinates (recipients) expect to hear. We can then turn these expectations to our advantage in improving communication and at the same time avoid the shock that accompanies our attempt to make the recipients "change their mind" or perceive what they do not expect to perceive.

Communication Makes Demands

The highest readership of any item in the daily American newspaper is enjoyed by the syndicated columns of two sisters: *Dear Abby* (Abigail van Buren) and Ann Landers. Why would anyone want to read these spicy self-confessionals? The answer is that these daily columns make no demands on the reader and we therefore have a case of excellent communication. We receive because there is a reward for doing so. Moreover, the message makes practically no demands upon our mental capacity.

Too many teachers fail to appreciate this principle. They demand retention, if not understanding, of historical dates, mathematical equations, financial ratios, and a blackboard of what the student considers to be minutiae. Real understanding is unlikely unless the recipient is provided with some motivation, some reason for learning. Communication has broken down. The learner shortly forgets because the mental demands of understanding and retention are too difficult.

If a message makes too many demands on the receiver, no communication occurs. On the other hand, the message will be received if it appeals to the receiver's motivation. If the communication fits in with the aspirations, values, or purposes of the recipient, it will likely be received in the form the sender intended. If it goes against these motivations, aspirations, or values, it will be resisted.

Communication and Information

When the U.S. Marine Corps drill sergeant barks: "Right face!" there is perfect communication because information exchange is perfect. Each command has only one possible meaning; it rests on preestablished understanding between sender and receiver regarding the specific response expected. Most formal information systems result in something less than the perfect communication exchange of the drill sergeant. Some company information systems serve to complicate rather than to enhance communication. We pay lip service to "management by exception" and demand concise reports that provide only information on the "critical variances." What we get is information overload or information blackout.

Information is always encoded. To be classified as communication the code must be understood by both the sender and receiver. This requires prior agreement on the code and to what the information pertains. This is not generally the case. The preparation of inputs for information reports is frequently misunderstood and is viewed as an unpleasant task at best. The output reports are rarely used because the information means different things to different people.

The problem with the vast majority of information is that it is formal and therefore impersonal. It depends on prior agreement on meaning and application. Communication, on the other hand, requires a human relationship. We therefore find ourselves in the unfortunate position of having an information explosion that widens the communication gap. The challenge is to close this gap by communicating on a human basis with information that is meaningful to superior and subordinate alike.

The Solution: Upward Communication Based on Results

For too long the superior–subordinate relationship has been based on the quicksand of insufficient information and vague goals. Exhortations to "sharpen up the operations" or "do a better job" or "get those costs down" are representative of communication at its worst. There is no message, no recipient, no perception, and no result.

Experience and common sense tell us that communication, motivation, and hence productivity can be improved by taking an approach which involves two fundamental ideas:

1. Start the communication process with the receiver, not the sender. This requires a philosophy of upward, rather than downward communication.

2. Focus upward communication on something that is common to sender and receiver, something that they both perceive alike. This is the expected result. This approach forces subordinates to think through logically and present to the superior their own ideas as to what contribution they are expected to make.

This communication by results approach provides a common perception between superior and subordinate, between sender and receiver, an essential requirement of good communication. Moreover the subordinate is provided access to a new relationship that provides the essential ingredients for motivation: participation in an understanding of the realities of decision making, a choice between what the situation demands and what one ordinarily would like to do, a new understanding of one's role and responsibility, and a breakthrough in organizational inflexibility.

CHECKLIST FOR SUBORDINATE
DEVELOPMENT AND COMMUNICATION

	Yes	No
1. Regarding "stretch" objectives for subordinates, have you:		
Identified the level of performance that will keep each subordinate in mild stress?	( )	( )
Translated this level of performance into result-focused goals?	( )	( )
Provided periodic feedback on progress and revised goals as necessary?	( )	( )
2. Do you practice the principles of the self-fulfilling prophecy by:		
Developing confidence in your job?	( )	( )
Developing confidence in your ability to develop subordinates?	( )	( )
Developing an ability to communicate expectations to subordinates?	( )	( )
3. Do you believe in the philosophy of upward communication and practice it?	( )	( )
4. Have you reviewed the company's and your formal channels of communication to determine which are effective?	( )	( )
5. Do you practice the four fundamentals of communication by results:		
Communication is perception?	( )	( )
Communication is expectations?	( )	( )
Communication makes demands?	( )	( )
Communication and information?	( )	( )

5

Managing Subordinates

Delegation and Control, Leadership Style, and Organizational Style

Delegation
Control
Leadership Style
Organizational Style
Evaluate Your Readiness for Control
and Leadership

A comment made by a supervisor in a Sony Corporation plant in the United States reflects an increasing American interest in the relationship between Japanese productivity and their managerial style. He remarked: "You get the feeling around here that they care about people, whereas in my previous work experience with U.S. companies they cared only about output and meeting the profit projections."

If this philosophy of management results in better productivity[1] perhaps we can learn a lesson from the Japanese. Five aspects of their approach are of interest: (1) emphasis on a flow of information and initiative from the bottom up; (2) making top management the facilitator of decisions rather than the issuer of edicts; (3) using middle management as the impetus for, and shaper of, solutions to problems; (4) stressing consensus as the way of making decisions; and (5) paying close attention to the well-being of employees.

Contrast this style with Western traditions of authority and hierarchy. The American supervisor is more inclined to resort to the typical trappings of authority delegation and control: the organization manual, position descriptions, activity charts, formal plans and programs, company policies, budgets, and procedures. Authority is almost always delegated downwards.

In this chapter we will examine the impact of authority delegation and subsequent control on productivity and how leadership and organizational styles affect results. I will argue that supervisory styles in all these areas should move slightly to the left of the classical, traditional approach which emphasizes structure and procedure.

DELEGATION

Studies of managerial failures almost invariably identify poor delegation as a major cause. Much of the reason for this lies in the manager's personal attitude and resulting inability to delegate. The manager confuses power with authority.

An extreme view of delegation is illustrated by the Army drill sergeant who announced: "Everything you are permitted to do will be ordered by

---

[1] In 1975 the U.S. Government National Commission on Productivity and Work Quality evaluated the applicability of Japanese management techniques within the U.S. system. Through examination of the productivity performance of identical semiconductor assembly lines in Houston, Texas, and in Tokyo, both of which were owned by the same American company, used the same tools, and employed the same number of workers, it was discovered that the plant in Tokyo outproduced Houston by 15 percent. In several other instances, Japanese managed companies in the U.S. were outperforming American companies in the same industries. For example, the absenteeism and turnover averages at a Japanese managed Sony plant in San Diego were from 25 to 50 percent lower than those of other electronics companies in the area. (From U.S. House of Representatives, *Hearings on the National Center for Productivity Act of 1975*. Washington, D.C.: Government Printing Office, 1975.)

me. Everything else is forbidden." Contrast this with the philosophy of a major division of the General Electric Company which states: "All authority not expressly and in writing reserved for higher management is granted to lower management."

Without delegation of authority, an organization would cease to exist. There would be only one department because the chief executive would be the only manager. It does no good to set up a structure of departmentalized activities unless authority is delegated to the units within the structure.

Authority delegation, like communication, is almost invariably downward. While this is the natural flow of authority, a good argument can be made that it is the job of upper management to support lower levels. After all, it is the front line supervisors who are on the "firing line" and responsible for getting the job done. They and their subordinates produce and design the product or service, make the sale, and perform the necessary auxiliary tasks. Thus, the higher-level manager has the job of supporting those on the firing line.

How to Delegate

Proper delegation can become a powerful motivator for productivity and job satisfaction. These six basic principles can go a long way toward overcoming the difficulty that most managers have in delegating.

1. *Delegate by results expected.* To do otherwise is to confuse the subordinate as to what is expected. Assignments and jobs must be defined in terms of what results are to be achieved. This will also permit a finer degree of planning and communication.

2. *Don't delegate upward* by passing the buck to the boss. The subordinate must be willing to accept authority and decision-making responsibility. Many top executives complain that their lower level managers view their jobs as one of pushing their problems upward. If you accept the responsibility for results or a decision, don't pass the buck upwards to the desk of the boss.

3. *Match responsibility with authority.* Responsibility, once accepted, is the obligation to achieve a result. Therefore, you cannot assign more responsibility to subordinates than they have the authority to carry out. In other words, assign responsibility in terms of results and delegate the necessary authority to meet it.

4. *Trust subordinates.* It is obvious that the manager who wants to delegate must be willing to release a certain amount of authority and decision-making rights to subordinates. It is said that the problem with most managers is that they "can't let go." When they are promoted they continue to perform the job they left. Others insist on approving the smallest detail of operations within their departments.

It is essential to trust subordinates (remember the Pygmalion Effect?).

Moreover, subordinates must be allowed to make mistakes. It is the cheapest form of learning, provided the mistake doesn't endanger the company or the subordinate's position. This approach, accompanied by coaching and counseling, is far better than discouraging subordinates by criticism, intimidation, harping, or hovering over them with constant checks on their work.

5. *Communicate.* Delegation doesn't mean abdication. Maintain open lines of communication so that subordinates have the information and feedback necessary to carry out the delegated authority.

6. *Maintain some control.* These should be broad controls or self-control as discussed in the next section.

CONTROL

If the manager could depend upon flawless execution of plans by a perfectly balanced organization, there would be no need for control because results would invariably be as expected. But plans and operations rarely remain on course, and control is needed to follow up on results.

Recently there has been a perceptible change in the control process. The trend is to modify or supplement traditional control with self-control by results management. Nevertheless, the traditional approach remains the most widespread method of control in the management of an organization.

Traditional Control

The process of control has historically been composed of three basic steps: (1) setting standards of performance; (2) measuring performance against these standards; and (3) correcting variances from standards and plans.

Setting standards of performance involves defining for personnel at all levels of the organization what is expected of them in terms of job performance. Hence standards are criteria that results can be measured against. These criteria can be quantitative (e.g., 10 percent increase in sales) or qualitative (e.g., maintain high level of employee morale). A frequently-used definition of a performance standard is a statement of conditions existing when a job is performed satisfactorily.

The usual yardstick or criteria for measuring performance against plan for an activity can be stated in terms of cost, time, quantity, or quality. For example, the unit cost of raw materials can be controlled in terms of cost per unit, and this standard would apply in the purchasing operation. Time is a standard for sales when performance is measured in terms of meeting sales quotas during established time periods (e.g., weeks, months). In manufacturing, the direct labor hours per unit of output in a process operation is a common quantity measure. Quality is a common measure in judging the acceptability of such factors as product specification, grades of product sold, and reject rates in quality control.

These are yardsticks and not areas of activity to be measured. Ideally, everyone in the company should have some standard so that they understand what is expected of them in terms of job performance.

Measuring performance against a standard is the second step in the control process. This measurement is usually in the form of a personal observation or some form of report—oral or written.

The oldest and most prevalent means of measuring performance is by personal observation. The shop supervisor is on the scene and can personally check the time, cost, and quality of the work under supervision. Sales managers visit sales offices or make calls with their sales representatives to observe performance personally. Advantages include the benefits of immediacy, personal direct contact, and first-hand observation of intangibles such as morale, personnel, development, or customer reaction.

Control and performance reporting is being done increasingly in written form. This is due in part to the accelerating use of computer-based information systems and related reporting techniques. These reports have the advantage of providing a permanent record, subject to periodic review by the manager and the subordinates.

The proliferation of computer printout and other type of report documentation presents managers with an unfortunate dilemma. On the one hand they are faced with increasing complexity in organization that seems to suggest more reports in order to maintain coordination and communication. On the other hand, the reports are not being used for these purposes. Instead they are more often than not ignored or go unused by the front line supervisor.

Correcting variances is the third step in the traditional control process. It does little good to set standards and measure performance unless corrections are made in order to get the plan back on course. Correcting variances can best be described in terms of the other basic functions of the manager:

1. *Plan*—recycle the process, review the plan, modify the goal, or change the standard.

2. *Organize*—examine the organization structure to determine whether it is reflected in standards, make sure that duties are well understood, reassign people if necessary.

3. *Staff*—improve selection, training, or assignment.

4. *Direct*—improve motivation, explain the job better, get agreement on the standard.

The Problem With Traditional Control

Previously I described how the chief executive of a major aerospace firm eliminated the company's computer based management information system (CBMIS) because people at the grass-roots level were swamped with control reports that had become meaningless. When asked what substitute the company was going to use, he said he was going to "put the man back in management" by substituting a system of "management by commitment" for the many unused control reports.

This incident illustrates a paradox in management control. On the one hand we have the capacity to grind out an explosion of meaningless data. On the other hand few of these data really communicate, let alone control.[2] There is the ever present danger of the system obscuring the purpose for which it was intended. The question is rarely asked: "What is the minimum amount of data required to control an event; that is, what do we need to know that will give us a reliable picture of results?"

A greater shortcoming with traditional control methods and reports is the coercive nature of the process. A review of the factors affecting productivity discussed in Chapter 3 will reveal that our classical approach to controlling operations is not motivational. If anything, it is a demotivator.

If people were committed to achieving results, control would be increasingly a matter between superior and subordinate and constant historical variance reporting would be reduced. This need for more self-control can be demonstrated by the growing number of service and "knowledge" workers whose performance doesn't lend itself to the traditional control measures of the hourly worker. Not only is it hard to measure the cost or contribution of these people but supervision by historical controls is hardly likely to work. No one can motivate them but themselves. They are the guardian of their own standards, performance, and objectives. They can only be productive if they are responsible for their own job.

Results Management and Self-control

Management by results and self-control does not infer the elimination of control reports but requires that they be forward-looking and provide the individuals with the information needed to measure their performance against a clearly understood goal.

Peter Drucker, in his book *Management: Tasks, Responsibilities, Practices*, lists seven specifications that controls must satisfy. These are shown in Table 5–1 along with a statement summarizing how they are met be results management and self-control. Readers can determine whether their existing control reports meet these specifications.

[2] Data must be distinguished from information. Data are facts and figures that are not being used to make decisions. They are historical records that are recorded and filed in support of some filing requirement or as backup for supporting documents. Information consists of data that have been retrieved, processed, or otherwise made ready for decision making, forecasting, or other operational use. The vast majority of "information systems" contain nothing more than data that is used for clerical purposes. For a discussion of problems in this regard and how to design a true information system see, Joel E. Ross, *Modern Management and Information Systems*. Reston, Va.: Reston Publishing Co., Inc., 1976.

Table 5–1.

Specification	Results Management and Self-control
Economical	Control effort is focused on what really counts: results. Trivia, information overload, and disinterest is reduced. You don't spend more on the control system than the pay-off from it.
Meaningful	Control is focused on key result areas rather than events or activities not significantly affecting the individual supervisor.
Appropriate	Measurement is against a specific performance rather than a total function or "universe." Control follows the "80/20" rule which concentrates on the 20 percent of the activities that provide 80 percent of the results.
Congruent	Reduces large quantities of detailed data that give a false sense of security and an illusion of accuracy.
Timely	The historical "reporting back" of traditional control reports is never timely enough to avoid the deviation before it occurs. Self-control helps to provide "feedforward" instead of "feedback." It forecasts deviations and permits corrective action before the deviation occurs.
Simple	Traditional control reports are frequently ignored because of complexity and reporting of activities outside the responsibility area of the individual. Self-control is easily understood because it is tailored to the individual.
Operational	Self-control is focused on action rather than historical information.

LEADERSHIP STYLE

There is almost universal agreement that individual productivity is significantly influenced by the superior–subordinate relationship in the work situation. This relationship can be productive or nonproductive depending on the leadership style of the superior. It is therefore important for all managers to examine their style and make changes if required. If changes cannot be made, managers can at least identify their style and understand what reaction it is likely to evoke on the part of subordinates.

Although everyone agrees that leadership is important, there is far less agreement on what constitutes good leadership or the content of leadership theory. Over time, a number of approaches have developed.

Approaches to Leadership

The *traitist* approach to leadership is the oldest and, to a large extent, the best known and most prevalent today, at least in terms of support by practicing managers. This theory can be traced back to the medieval period when Alfarabi identified the traits of a leader as intelligence, excellent memory, eloquence, firmness, and temperance. Later, in the 16th century, Niccolo Machiavelli wrote that leaders were born but could also be made and he identified charismatic personality as a requirement for ruling as a prince. Subsequent writers and researchers have identified and tested literally hundreds of additional traits such as initiative, judgment, moral courage, perseverance, endurance, and so on. The list is endless.

There are two problems with the traitist approach to leadership. First, there is no evidence that any trait or group of traits correlate with productivity and results. Second, if an individual manager lacks these "born" traits, there isn't much chance that he can develop them. In conclusion, the traitist approach doesn't offer us much help in terms of an operational answer to productivity.

The Theory X and Theory Y approach of Douglas McGregor[3] is currently enjoying widespread attention. The theory identifies two extreme styles along a continuum, thus:

$$\longrightarrow \qquad\qquad\qquad\qquad\qquad\qquad\qquad \longrightarrow$$

Theory X	Theory Y
(Autocratic)	(Participative)
Traditional	Human Relations

Theory X assumes that people are lazy, dislike and shun work, have to be driven, and need the carrot and the stick. This assumption says that most people are incapable of taking responsibility for themselves and should be looked after, presumably by the leader. By contrast, Theory Y makes the assumption that workers have a psychological need to work and want responsibility so that they can achieve. The manager should therefore locate his style closer to Theory Y along the continuum if required.

Perhaps one of the major contributions of McGregor's theory has been to highlight the inescapable fact that the traditional Theory X approach to leadership no longer works. Theory Y, on the other hand, does not give us an operational approach that fulfills our requirement for making work productive and the worker achieving. In other words, we know that Theory X

---

[3] Douglas McGregor, *The Human Side of Enterprise*. New York: McGraw–Hill, 1960. This book contained the original idea of Theory X and Theory Y. Since that time numerous other authors have popularized the theory.

doesn't work but we aren't sure how to put Theory Y to work on the job. It is not enough to merely adopt a participative philosophy. Something else is needed.

The *style* approach to leadership has also been very popular. Researchers have attempted to identify the characteristics present in styles of leadership behavior (e.g., autocratic, democratic, paternalistic, participative, custodial, supportive, collegial, and so on) and the impact of each style on organizational behavior. In management seminars, participants are asked to identify these types of behavior and the impact of the leadership style on subordinates with such questions as: "What would be your reaction to this style?" or "Under what conditions would this style be appropriate?"

There are two significant shortcomings to the style approach. First, it doesn't resolve the apparent conflict between task orientation and people orientation, despite the fact that task relationships and people relationships are not mutually exclusive. Second, the approach doesn't tell us how productivity can be achieved by results management and motivation. Somewhat like the traitist approach, the style approach leaves us with little more than a general impression of subordinate reaction to a given style.

The *situational* (or contingency) approach says that successful leadership is a function of: (1) the forces in the leaders; (2) the characteristics of and types of needs of subordinates; and (3) the situation. Forces in the leader might include the person's value system, confidence in subordinates, inclination in terms of leadership style, and perception of how power and authority should be used. Subordinate characteristics and needs might include education and training, interest in the work, and group values. The situation for the practice of leadership is almost unlimited. It involves the nature of the work, level of management, organizational policies, problems to be solved, and environment.

While the situational or contingency approach cannot be denied (because it includes all possible variables), a casual examination will reveal that the interaction of these forces, variables, and situations present the manager with an infinite and therefore impossible array of leadership situations. Understanding requires almost universal genius on the part of the manager. Most of us find it hard enough to know what we need to know about some technical area of expertise (e.g., accounting, engineering, sales, manufacturing) without the added problem of becoming a psychologist.

What is needed is a simple *operational* approach to leadership, one that achieves productivity by making the worker achieve. As background for the identification of such a style, it is desirable to set out some requirements for good leadership.

Requirements for Good Leadership

From the foregoing discussion and what we know about the topic, we can discredit two old myths. One is that there is one best leadership style, or that there are leaders who excel under all circumstances. The other is that some persons are born leaders, and that neither training, experience, or conditions can materially affect leadership skills.

By saying what leadership is *not* doesn't tell us what it *is*. But if productivity is what we are seeking, then we can list a number of general requirements that have emerged over time. To be an effective leader, the manager should be able to:

1. *Resolve conflict* before it can become damaging to cooperation, organizational integration, and achievement of results. A major reason why conflict develops in organizations is that people do not understand the results expected of them or their co-workers.

2. *Allow participation* in decisions for the common good, not for "permissiveness" or for reasons of "human relations."

3. *Encourage creativity and innovation* in work methods that provide better results in terms of subordinate fulfillment and achievement.

4. *Manage by results* based on upward communication and establishment of goals by subordinates.

5. *Provide control and feedback* that fulfills the requirements of: (a) clear understanding of results expected; (b) information on progress; and (c) information for self-monitoring and control.

6. *Maintain morale* that is grounded in good performance and not paternalism, human relations, or some "happiness index." Focus is on opportunities and not problems.

7. *Negotiate and maintain commitment* to goals that are established in the superior subordinate relationship. Results depend on commitment, not lip service.

8. *Set stretch objectives* that require subordinates to "reach out" for productivity and satisfaction.

9. *Develop subordinates* by providing opportunities for growth.

10. *Utilize appraisal* as an opportunity for setting future objectives rather than focusing on reward or punishment based on past performance that is judged on traits.

11. The final requirement for a good leader is that his style and behavior should have a *positive impact on organizational longevity and growth.*

The Results Management Style of Leadership

If the above requirements truly represent what we expect from a good leader, then we can examine an approach to leadership that may give us an operational answer to how we can achieve productivity while fulfilling these requirements.

Two psychologists, Robert Blake and Jane Mouton, have originated an approach to leadership styles that has gained widespread acceptance. It is known as The Managerial Grid.®[4] This innovative "school" of effective leadership behavior attempts to integrate the three basic "universals" of organizational life: (1) the need for production; (2) the need for satisfaction on the part of organizational members; and (3) the inevitable hierarchy of authority, the *boss* aspect of getting results. Blake and Mouton also attempt to balance the two ends of the managerial continuum that emphasize production on the one hand (Theory X) and people on the other (Theory Y). The basic contention is that organizational goals and satisfaction of worker's needs are not incompatible.

Figure 5–1 is the original Managerial Grid® figure. It identifies five leadership styles depending upon the manager's concern for production (results) and people (motivation). For a discussion of leadership styles, we can construct a model such as the one shown in Figure 5–2. As you can see there are eighty-one (9 x 9) "styles" on the grid but the five extremes are identified and discussed below for illustration.

9,1 The Task Style These managers believe that there is a contradiction between production and the personal needs of people and since their concern is almost totally with production, they resolve this contradiction in favor of output. They are exacting taskmasters and achieve results by not permitting the human element to interfere. They know how to use their authority; they use it to coerce compliance. They represent the true *autocrat*, the "carrot and stick" type of manager.

1,9 The Country Club Style These managers, somewhat like the 9,1 style, believe that the requirements for production and results are contrary to the needs of people. Unlike the 9,1 manager, they resolve the conflict in favor of people because to them, people come first. They arrange for the "happiness" of their subordinates by providing a comfortable and friendly atmosphere with a work tempo to match. They view themselves as the boss but don't use their authority to pressure subordinates. They lead by following. They are *paternalistic* leaders and have a high concern for the morale of "their" people.

1,1 The Impoverished Style These managers are usually found in some unimportant staff job or where operations have settled into a programmed routine. They assume that there is incompatibility between production and people needs but they have little concern for either. They are apathetic and self-defeating and summarize their supervisory role as, "I don't want to get involved." They think the best way to lead is to lead least and therefore they encourage subordinates to "do it your way." If

[4] R. R. Blake and J. S. Mouton, *The Managerial Grid*. Houston: Gulf Publishing Company, 1964, page 10.

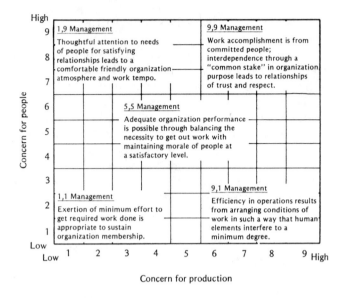

Figure 5–1. The Managerial Grid®
Source: R. R. Blake and J. S. Mouton, *The Managerial Grid*. Houston: Gulf Publishing Company, 1964, p. 10. Reproduced with permission.

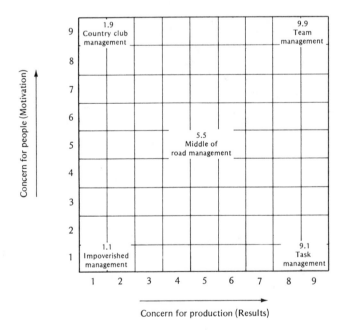

Figure 5–2. Styles of Leadership

forced to make a decision they will do it "by the book." They are waiting out retirement and social security. Oddly enough, these managers are frequently very highly motivated by activities unrelated to their jobs.

5,5 Middle of the Road Style These managers are excellent politicians and are fast on their feet. They believe that production and the needs of people are conflicting and view their job as resolving this conflict through negotiating, persuasion, and selling their own solutions. Since an imbalance exists between the need for results and the needs of people, they spend much of their time orchestrating an "in-between" position that is not the optimum for either requirement. They see themselves as motivator and communicator rather than as boss. If unable to resolve conflict they will take a vote. They are democratic bosses. They are usually firm but fair. They are *democratic*.

9,9 Team Management Unlike the other four leadership styles, the 9,9 managers see no inherent conflict between production and the needs of people. On the contrary, they believe that the needs of people can best be met by giving them an opportunity for achievement. They know that production is in everyone's interest.

The 9,9 manager is *participative* but not in any paternalistic sense. Nor is participation a means for sharing responsibility or authority relationships. It is a means for organizing subordinate responsibility and achievement. The 9,9 managers view their role as establishing the conditions that integrate the potential for subordinate achievement and motivation through team action that is focused on *results*.

Summary: Integrating Leadership
Requirements and Leadership Styles

In chapter 3 I outlined nine factors that affect productivity in the work situation: challenging work, participation in decisions, compensation tied to performance, communication, supervision, recognition, self-development, stewardship, and organization style.

In this chapter I have established ten general requirements for good leadership: conflict resolution, decision making, creativity and innovation, management by results, delegation and control, maintenance of morale, negotiation and maintenance of commitment to goals, setting stretch objectives, appraisal, and subordinate development. Additionally, I said that another requirement for a good leader was to have a positive impact on organizational longevity and growth.

The conclusion should emerge at this point that the real job of the leader is to provide those factors that affect productivity by meeting the requirements of good leadership.

Table 5-2 compares these requirements with the five styles of leadership. An examination of Table 5-2 should convince the reader that, in

Table 5-2. Comparison of Leadership Requirements and Styles

STYLE OF LEADERSHIP	Resolution Of Conflict	Decision Making	Creativity & Innovation	Philosophy of Results Management	Maintains Morale	Negotiates Commitment
9,1 TASK (Produce or Perish)	Suppresses or stamps it out. Establishes "win-lose" confrontation in which he/she always wins. Conflict simmers under surface.	Inner-directed. Subordinates not capable of participation. Makes decisions and enforces them.	"I am the boss and only I have the capability and responsibility to innovate."	Frequent demands to "get results" but these are not identified. Avoids joint goal setting and upward communication. No feedback.	Believes in tight supervision and "keep busy" syndrome.	None. Subordinate reactions are 1,1 behavior or militancy or sabotage.
1,9 COUNTRY CLUB	Smoothes it over in order to relieve tension.	Solicits ideas of others in order to gain acceptance or avoid unpopular decision.	None expected and none encouraged except those that make work easier or "happier." Productivity is not the objective.	Approves because it is viewed as technique to lower supervision requirements. Sets "pseudo" but not organization goals.	Morale is primary focus and believes in taking care of "my people." Human relations oriented.	Committed to human relations and not goals. Desires subordinate commitment to "I like it here" attitude.
1,1 IMPOVERISHED	Avoids if at all possible. If forced to resolve, will resort to "the book" on company policy or procedure.	Avoids occasions for decisions. Defers to others. As a last resort, consults "the book."	Unrelated to company or productivity goals. May be quite innovative outside the work environment.	Avoids!	People are happiest when left alone.	None to boss. Goal is "stay out of trouble." OK to pursue own private goals.
5,5 MIDDLE OF THE ROAD	Firm but fair attitude. Attempts to "cool off" conflict or reach compromise.	Compromises or sells his decision or takes a vote to get majority rule.	Encouraged unless it results in threatening conditions.	Generally approves but is faced with dichotomy when he can't reconcile personal goals with organization goals.	Attempts to "balance" morale and productivity. Measures morale by opinion survey or "happiness index."	Believes he is "go-between" to promote the company way. Attempts to sell commitment.
9,9 TEAM MANAGEMENT (People Support What They Participate in)	Gets the facts in the open and solves conflict based on how it is affecting results.	Gets best decision from team (group) on how to get results. Decisions based on facts and rational approach.	Encouraged for productivity and hence group goals. Innovation is motivation.	Views it as the central vehicle and basic philosophy for motivation and productivity.	Motivation is self-actualization through having a stake in results. Believes in team effort.	Has a sense of organizational purpose. Organization goals are same as personal goals. Negotiates commitment.

STYLE OF LEADERSHIP	Feedback & Control	Sets Stretch Objectives	Develops Subordinates	Appraisal	Long-Term Impact of Leadership Style on Organization
9,1 TASK (Produce or Perish)	Sets tight quotas and schedules with no participation. Frequent checking. Feedback after the fact and mostly for the "bad news."	Ratchet principle.	Believes human relations are soft. Development confined to training in company rules and procedures.	"Shape up or ship out."	1,1 behavior. Underutilization of people.
1,9 COUNTRY CLUB	Avoids specific standards and promotes "general" goals that everyone can support.	Sets mild stretch goals if they are "comfortable" and morale doesn't suffer.	Development devoted to "fitting in" or "getting acquainted." Uses company activities such as recreation indoctrination.	"How can I help my subordinates lead a rewarding life?"	OK for cost plus or monopoly situation. Ultimate result of "fat and happy" attitude is going broke.
1,1 IMPOVERISHED	Avoids both goals and controls. "I just want to make it to retirement."	Let the subordinates set their own. But don't bother me.	Nonexistent. Sends subordinates to development activities to "fill the quota." Attends personally only if nominated.	Comply with company appraisal policy and system. Appraise not too high and not too low. Avoid confrontation.	The classic bureaucracy.
5,5 MIDDLE OF THE ROAD	Balances personal and organization goals. Meets about 75 percent of targets.	Mild if acceptable to subordinate.	Pays lip service but not convinced. Believes organization and product knowledge is more important.	"I want my subordinates to go away from the appraisal interview with a good feeling."	OK if goal is to maintain the status quo but not if growth and innovation is desired.
9,9 TEAM MANAGEMENT (People Support What They Participate in)	Organization and individual goals are the same. Manage by self-control.	Yes. Mild stress through "reach out" goals is self-development and self-actualization.	Believes in organization development. Learn by doing. Self-development through increasing responsibility.	Appraisal is opportunity to negotiate goal commitment, provide feedback, and develop subordinates.	Sustained growth for the organization and its members.

Each of the following items describes some aspect of your relationship with your employees. Reach each item and then circle the response [1, 2, 3, 4, 5] which most nearly reflects the extent of your agreement or disagreement. Try to respond according to the way you would actually handle the situation on the job.

The best way to get good performance out of employees is to . . . .

	Response				
	Agree com-pletely (1)	Mostly agree (2)	Par-tially agree (3)	Mostly dis-agree (4)	Disagree com-pletely (5)
1. Allow them extensive freedom to plan and organize their own work.	1	2	3	4	5
2. Allow employees to set up special meet-ings and other ways to work out their differences and conflicts.	1	2	3	4	5
3. Not give them information unrelated to their immediate work.	1	2	3	4	5
4. Spell out exactly what their jobs are and what is expected of them.	1	2	3	4	5
5. Always insist that they solve their own work problems, but be available as a consulting resource to them.	1	2	3	4	5
6. Maintain tight controls on all work to be sure things don't get out of line.	1	2	3	4	5
7. Provide time, money and other resources so each person can develop| his particular strengths and capabili-ties to the fullest.	1	2	3	4	5
8. Set up systems where information on performance results goes directly to the employee instead of through you.	1	2	3	4	5
9. Discourage employees from getting involved in the "why" of doing their job.	1	2	3	4	5

Figure 5-3. Readiness Questionnaire

Source: Glenn H. Varney, *Management by Objectives*. Chicago: The Dartnell Corporation, 1971. Used by permission.

general, productivity can best be achieved by a 9,9 managerial style. This is a general conclusion and, of course, does not apply in all situations.

Evaluate Your Readiness
For Results Management

If you are interested in productivity and think that a results management approach can help achieve it, you may want to begin thinking of your managerial style. An indication of this style can be obtained by completing the questionnaire contained in Figure 5-3. After completing the question-

Response

	Agree completely (1)	Mostly agree (2)	Partially agree (3)	Mostly disagree (4)	Disagree completely (5)
10. Bring employees together in joint meetings to make decisions and solve mutual problems.	1	2	3	4	5
11. Give them full information about their jobs, the department and the company.	1	2	3	4	5
12. Tell employees where they are going wrong and convince them of the merits of changing their attitudes and approaches.	1	2	3	4	5
13. Solve problems for employees as quickly as possible so they can get back to work.	1	2	3	4	5
14. Allow employees to take the responsibility for controlling and managing their own work.	1	2	3	4	5
15. Encourage employees to redesign their jobs around their own capabilities.	1	2	3	4	5
16. Leave employees alone and count on them to get their jobs done.	1	2	3	4	5
17. Clamp down on conflict and friction between employees.	1	2	3	4	5
18. Train employees to do their work according to standard procedures.	1	2	3	4	5
19. Insist that employees stick to their jobs and leave decisions and planning to you.	1	2	3	4	5
20. Discourage employees from introducing new ways of doing their work without first checking with you.	1	2	3	4	5

Instructions for Scoring: (1) Circle these questions: 1, 2, 5, 7, 8, 10, 11, 14, 15, and 16. Score 1 point for each response that was a 1 or 2. Add up your score and enter under the S/J heading in Figure 5-4. (2) For the remainder of the questions, score 1 point for each response that was a 4 or 5. Enter the score under the S/S heading, Figure 5-4.

Figure 5–3. (continued).

naire, you can score yourself according to the scoring key which is provided and enter your score on Readiness Profile shown in Figure 5–4.

If you score close to the Readiness Range or in the Readiness Range on the S/J scale, this indicates the way in which you perceive your employees working under such a system and means that you are on the right track in terms of your perception of how your subordinates are going to perform their jobs. If you score high on the S/S, this indicates the way in which you actually manage.

The S/S and S/J scales are not necessarily in line. For example, if S/S is lower than S/J, you might review the things you do in managing

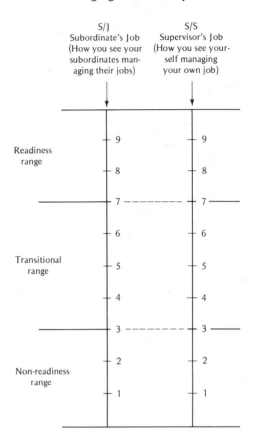

Figure 5–4. Results Management Readiness Profile

your subordinates which may be contradictory to what you have told them you would like them to do.

If S/S is higher than S/J, it may mean that although you are willing to manage by results, you may not be setting the environment in which this is taking place.

ORGANIZATION STYLE

The company's organizational structure and the balance between the several activities within the company are basic determinants of productivity. Costly resources are wasted if people are unclear about organizational relationships. Time is lost if employees waste it in trying to find out what they are supposed to do rather than doing it.

Many managers handle their physical and financial resources acceptably but overlook the cost of human resources that result from poor organizational dynamics. For most companies, payrolls are running around eight times earnings, so it becomes obvious that an increase of, say five percent in the productivity of employees through better organization would have a really significant impact.

The Classical Bureaucratic Structure

This style was discussed at some length in chapter 2 and we pointed out how the "evils" of bureaucracy could be overcome in part by results management. Lest the reader conclude that the classical design is all bad, let me caution at this point that bureaucracy, with all of its "evils," is an organizational requirement in most cases. It has the advantages of clarity, structure, and stability. But the price for these advantages are the drawbacks listed in chapter 2; it is nonadaptive, hinders communication, inhibits innovation, relies on coercive control, and encourages make-work, as well as incompatible goals between an organization and its members.

Despite the criticisms frequently leveled at it, this basic structure will probably be around for a long time to come. Not long ago, a survey of the Fellows of the Academy of Management, a group of distinguished senior management professors, attempted to forecast the shape of the organization of the future. The overwhelming conclusion was that the dominant organizational structure in 1985 will still be the classic pyramid. The problem is how to make it work in spite of itself.

This discussion should not lead the reader to the conclusion that the choice of organizational styles can be reduced to an "either-or" answer either classical or some other form. Whatever form we adopt, it will be a modification of the basic classical structure with its functional grouping of specialized skills.

The Behavioral Model

The behavioral scientists have been the most persistent critics of the classical structure. Their basic quarrel is that it is too mechanistic and therefore tends to overlook human nature and the needs of people. Some maintain that organizational trappings such as procedure and controls actually violate human needs and inhibit productivity; others contend that the pyramid style, although suitable for a stable environment, is unable to accommodate the change that is characteristic of modern companies.

In the behavioral model an attempt is made to overcome some of the mechanistic–structural objections. The model assumes the objective of economic productivity output as given, but it adds a new dimension—

employee satisfaction. This satisfaction, which presumably leads to greater productivity, is a function not so much of structure as of individual perception and personal value systems.

Essentially, the idea is that the pyramid should be modified to provide:

1. A more democratic attitude on the part of managers.

2. More participation in major decisions at lower levels.

3. Decentralization of decision making as far as possible.

4. Less emphasis on hierarchy and authority delegation.

5. Less narrow specialization of tasks.

Most managers react to the approach in one of four ways: with skepticism; with a pretense of acceptance but an actual intention to manipulate people and decisions; with general agreement but confusion about how to implement the model; or with an enthusiastic desire to adopt the philosophy as a modern way to motivate people. Among those who seem to be committed to this approach is a Chrysler vice president who said: "Let responsibility extend down to its lowest practical level and give authority to go along with it. The lowest level in a lot of cases is the guy right on the line."

At Chrysler, assembly workers in selected plants were authorized to reject substandard parts, work sitting instead of standing, and paint their machines any color they wish. Other companies that reflect this approach include AT&T, where selected typists can now research, compose, and sign their own letters without supervision. Many other companies have tried a variety of job enrichment programs where assembly workers who formerly performed very specialized tasks now assemble components or entire products and approve the final checkout.

There is a lot of talk about the behavioral approach to organizational style and its effect on productivity. It is more of a philosophy of motivation than an organization structure. But when combined with a management by results approach it promises wider acceptance.

Situational Approach

This view of organization design seeks to answer the question of what factors, forces, or variables should be considered in deciding how to build the structure. The most important variables are:

The manager Since people, not organizations, have objectives, the value system, philosophy, and objectives of top management have an impact on organizational design. How do they view the freedom of the individual to make decisions? How do they feel about normal authority channels? How do they view the interaction between the company and its external environment? These are questions that shape the views of the managers and hence the organization.

The work The nature of the tasks required to achieve organizational goals (the real reason for organizing) determines the shape of the structure. In a mature, single process industry, such as steel, there would be less need for an adaptive structure than there would be in an emerging technology industry such as aerospace.

The environment Social, political, economic, and technological factors in the environment and the degree to which the company interacts with that environment will have an impact on the design of the organizational structure. The more complexity and interaction, the more impact it will have.

The individual contributors The human element is an essential factor. Growing evidence indicates that increased productivity and other desirable organizational outputs can be achieved by adapting the structure to accommodate the needs of organizational members.

The problem with this theory of design is the same that we had with the situational approach to leadership; the number of variables and the possible interactions between them make it difficult to *operationalize*. Although a careful evaluation of the contingencies of design would prove productive at the company level, it may prove difficult for the front-line supervisor.

The Team

The real organizational problem, at least at the level of the front-line supervisor or middle manager, is to balance the existing functional structure with its skill specialization against the organization of people and tasks necessary to achieve results, to "break through" the pyramid, so to speak. The answer to this paradox appears to lie in the team approach to organization style. This approach complements the classical structure to functional grouping (the employee's "home") with a work team (the employee's "place of work"). Committees, expeditors, departmental meetings, and the like are not teams. The team organization is not a temporary expedient to solve a special short-run problem. It involves a design principle all its own.

The classical bureaucracy, which we have agreed cannot be abandoned, is traditionally based upon one of two design principles concerned with work. First, you can organize the work by project, stages, or some form of work breakdown such as the development of a product or the construction of a plant. Second, you can bring the work to where the skills and tools can be applied to it. An example of this is the assembly line where cutting, welding, assembly, and painting can take place.

In the team style of organization, you take the workers with different skills, tools, and competencies and move them to the job to be done. I have frequently experienced this style of organization when functioning as a lecturer in educational television productions. The team—the director, lecturer, the graphic artist, the camera operators, the set designer—works as a team, although each does highly specialized work.

The team form of organization is not new. The task force and project manager have been around for years. IBM has always encouraged workers to form teams within the mass production system. But, the use of teams is growing. The automobile industry has been experimenting on the assembly line. The use of product managers and project managers is growing increasingly popular in industry. The venture team concept is a recent innovation developed to meet the demand for a breakthrough in product design and marketing. Genenral Electric, always an innovator, has reorganized the entire firm around 63 "SBUs"—Strategic Business Units. At Texas Instruments, team management is a way of life and has been carried to a high degree of sophistication. Several hundred "TAPs"—tactical action programs—were organized to achieve company strategy and goals. Motorola has pushed decentralization down to the plant level where product managers develop their own strategy and product plans. Ralston Purina has local decision-making work groups right on the shop floor to innovate in work standards and methods. A few companies have organized "productivity teams."

The team approach to organization style offers the front-line supervisor and middle manager, whether line or staff, an alternative to the classical structure, or rather, a modification to it in order to achieve productivity. However, it is not a panacea nor does it apply in all situations. It is not generally appropriate by itself but must be complementary to the existing structure.

It is a challenge for managers to determine for themselves how the team concept of organizational style can be applied to get results in a particular situation.

EVALUATE YOUR READINESS
FOR CONTROL AND LEADERSHIP

	Yes	No
1. Do you practice these principles of delegation:		
Delegate by results expected?	( )	( )
Don't pass the buck upward?	( )	( )
Match authority with responsibility?	( )	( )
Trust subordinates?	( )	( )
Maintain open lines of communication?	( )	( )

*If no, review the benefits and techniques
to achieve productivity by delegation.*

	Yes	No
2. Do you use formal controls as a "crutch" or as a tool to coerce subordinates?	( )	( )

*If yes, try results management and
self control.*

	Yes	No
3. Do your controls and reports meet the seven requirements of economical, meaningful, appropriate, congruent, timely, simple, and operational?	( )	( )

*If no, revision of formal controls
is probably in order.*

	Yes	No
4. Do you subscribe to one of the classical approaches to leadership: traitist, style, or situational?	( )	( )

*If yes, you might review the concept of
productivity through self actualization
by results and self control.*

	Yes	No
5. Are you a 9,9 team management leader?	( )	( )

*If no, reaffirm for yourself how this
style of leadership best fullfills the
requirement for productivity.*

6. Do you find that the company's organization style
and structure gets in the way of coordination,
cooperation, and results?   ( ) ( )

*If yes, look into a modification by using
the team form of organizational style.*

6

Management by Objectives

The System for Achieving Results

Objectives
Hierarchy of Objectives
MBO as a System for Getting Results
Summary: Making MBO Work
Are You Ready for MBO?

Thus far I have argued that the systems approach and its fundamental concept of focus on results is the primary route to improved management in the organization. In this chapter we will examine a method for implementing a systems approach. It is called *management by objectives*. It is also called variously by such terms as management by results, participation, or commitment. Hereafter I will simply call it MBO.

MBO is far and away the most prevalent approach to the emerging discipline of organizational development and is the most pervasive managerial system of the 1970s. Literally thousands of companies around the world are practicing various styles of MBO. This chapter is not an exhaustive treatment of the subject but is sufficient for understanding and practice. Since the behavioral science foundation has already been laid in previous chapters, we will focus on the structural methodology.

Peter Drucker first coined the term "management by obectives" and in his recent book *Management* he calls it a philosophy of management:

> ". . . management by objectives and self control may properly be called a philosophy of management. It rests on a concept of the job of management. It rests on an analysis of the specific needs of the management group and the obstacles it faces. It rests on a concept of human action, behavior, and motivation. Finally, it applies to every manager, whatever his level and function and to any organization whether large or small. It insures performance by converting objective needs into personal goals."[1]

Drucker is correct. Results management and MBO are new and different ways of management. For many managers it calls for a reorientation of thinking, a different set of assumptions about how human resources should be utilized within an organization, and a new concept of delegation and control.

Utilization of the MBO concept does not depend entirely upon the installation of a formal company-wide system. Individual managers can develop objectives for themselves or for the work groups for which they are responsible. Their individual "mini systems" would introduce priorities, furnish internal feedback, and trigger results-directed behavior. However, a much better foundation would be provided by a system throughout the organization. This would assure that everyone's obectives would be consistent with and support those of the total company.

On the other hand, MBO is not a panacea. Many companies have installed formal systems that have failed. In almost every case this has been the result of emphasis on the system rather than on results. The cause has been lack of management support and follow-up.

[1] Drucker, *op. cit.*, p. 441.

OBJECTIVES

Many managers pay lip service to objectives and when asked will declare: "Of course, we manage by objectives." But when pressed, they are unable to define their objectives, let alone devise a plan to achieve them. Such platitudes as "increase market share" or "improve the operations" or "reduce turnover" reflect a catch-as-catch-can approach.

These managers may have a financial plan, or a rudimentary form of development plan but it is not enough. In almost every case you will find that managers and supervisors at lower levels are at best unclear and at worst totally unaware of company goals. It is unlikely that this environment will give us the two benefits of the systems approach: focus on results and organizational integration.

A simple definition of the work objective would be phrased in terms of *results expected*. It can also be defined as a temporary estimate of a desirable future result that cannot be predicted with accuracy that you are willing and able to pay for and that you believe can be achieved through effort. This definition focuses on a commitment to resources in order to achieve results. It therefore infers a more formal approach than a mere statement that "sure, we manage by objectives." I can't imagine a manager who would admit to not having an objective. What we need is a system to achieve those objectives.

HIERARCHY OF OBJECTIVES

Despite the inhibiting structure inferred by the word hierarchy, the *integrative* requirement demanded by MBO is achieved through the concept of the hierarchy of objectives. This implies that objectives are arranged in descending order much like the lines of authority shown on the organization chart. Assuming that the Board of Directors or the chief executive have established broad, overall company goals, these can be broken down into lower-level supporting objectives. The result may be imagined as a "cascade effect."

The entire system of MBO depends upon the eventual integration of closely understood company objectives at the top. Once again, you are reminded that platitudes will not suffice. Statements like "be a better supplier" or "have the best product in the industry" are not meaningful and cannot be divided into smaller increments for meaningful goals at lower levels. Objectives must be operational; they must be capable of being converted into specific targets and assignments at lower levels.

Many companies have followed Drucker's advice and have set overall company objectives in these eight key result areas:

1. *Marketing.* Following a clear determination of strategy (product, market scope, and competitive edge), objectives should be set for existing and new products and services in both existing and new markets. These include related objectives and policies such as distribution, service, pricing, and so on.

2. *Innovations* in management, product, and social requirements.

3. *Human organization and resources* including the basic structure, policies, and management of the business. Also, worker attitude, union relations, managerial development, and performance.

4. *Financial resources* concerned with the supply and utilization of capital.

5. *Physical resources* concerned with physical facilities, fixed assets, and raw material.

6. *Productivity* measurements for comparing management of different units within the company as well as the company with others in the industry regarding the productivity of land, labor, capital, and overall productivity.

7. *Social responsibility* related to the company's existence within the society and the economy.

8. *Profitability* in terms of earnings per share, return on investment, or some other measure.

The goals of employees' jobs are defined in terms of the contribution they have to make to the success of the larger unit of which they are a part. It is therefore clear that, whatever objectives are established, at any level, it is important to be as specific and accurate as possible. The multiplier effect of an inaccurate goal at a higher level can be demonstrated by the principle of "cumulative compounding of error." For example, you may think that ninety percent accuracy in goals is reasonable but at the end of a twelve step sequential process of goal setting (twelve levels down the hierarchy) ninety percent gets to be twenty-five percent. Eighty percent gets to be six percent and so on.

The "cascade effect" of establishing objectives at the top and converting them into increments at lower levels in the organization can be seen in Figure 6-1. In this particular breakdown, objectives are organized around these areas:

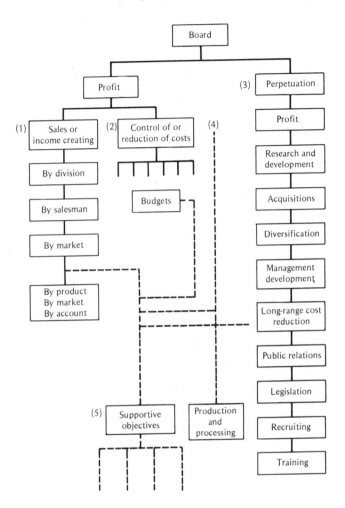

Figure 6–1. The "Cascade Effect" of a Hierarchy of Objectives

Sales or income creating.

Control of and reduction of costs.

Perpetuation of the organization.

Production and processing.

Supportive objectives.

Figure 6–2 illustrates another breakdown by organizational hierarchy. Each goal supports a higher goal of which it is a part.

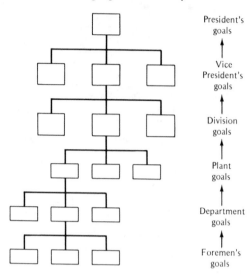

Figure 6–2. The Hierarchy of Objectives

MBO AS A SYSTEM FOR GETTING RESULTS

Three major arguments have been advanced thus far in this book. Chapters 3 and 4 should have convinced you that it is entirely possible to integrate or reconcile the organization's objectives that are concerned with results and productivity (growth, profitability, cost reduction, and so on) with the individual's own needs. MBO is the system than can achieve this. It can balance the company's goals with the individual's needs to contribute and develop personally. If this can be done, everyone has the best of both worlds.

A second argument that has been made is that the manager can set the proper climate for motivation, job satisfaction, and productivity through these results management methods:

Job development

Appraisal

Subordinate development

Communication

Delegation and control

Organization style

Leadership style

A third point that has been made is the lack of organizational integration (synergism) provided by the classical or traditional bureaucratic organization form.

Stated simply, MBO is the system that provides the central element in all three of the foregoing requirements. It is a system of productivity management that integrates:

1. Organization and individual goals.

2. The managerial requirements for results management.

3. The subsystems of the organization.

How the MBO System Works

In Figure 2–1, we constructed a system of productivity management that included the components of input, processor, and output. The Management by Objectives System can be depicted in the same manner. Figure 6–3 shows the components of the system, the output of which is results. Other components include input (define the job, define expected results), control (measure results), and feedback (appraisal). These are explained:

1. *Define the job.* Specification of the key responsibilities and duties for which the individual is held accountable.

2. *Define expected results (objectives).* The performance conditions (expressed in measurable, verifiable terms) that exist when the job is performed satisfactorily.

3. *Measure the results.* Comparison of the actual results achieved against the established objective.

4. *Appraisal.* The process of providing feedback on results and establishing the necessary modification to the job or the objectives in order to set expected results for the next performance period.

These basic four steps constitute the MBO *performance improvement cycle* for the individual. The cycle is repeated as often as necessary to maintain the desired level of productivity through the "stretch" performance process. Taken together, the performance improvement cycles of all the individuals in the organization comprise the route by which the total organization achieves its own goals. Without such a central integrating system, it is unlikely that the goals of the organization and those of its members will be in harmony. This concept of the route to growth and productivity for both individuals and the organization as a whole is shown in Figure 6–4.

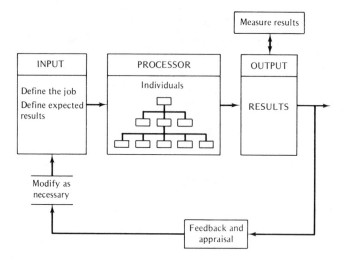

Figure 6–3.   The Management by Objectives System

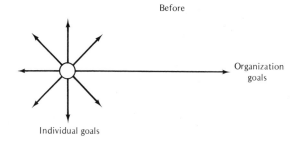

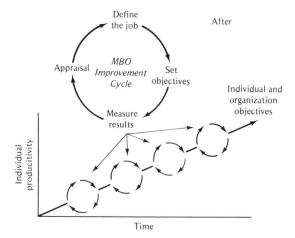

Figure 6–4.   Before and After the MBO Improvement Cycle

Defining the Job

A number of years ago the American Management Associations conducted a survey among hundreds of superior–subordinate teams to determine whether common agreement existed between superior and subordinate regarding job responsibilities. The result of the survey indicated widespread disagreement. Indeed, the area of agreement was extremely narrow. The superiors' concepts of their subordinate's duties differed substantially from what the subordinates thought about the matter. Subsequent studies have supported the conclusion that millions of people are not clear about what they are expected to do.

Vague understanding of job definition is generally attributable to: (1) job descriptions that are stated in general rather than specific terms; (2) job descriptions that are "programmed" to such an extent that no flexibility in job definition is permitted; and (3) the total lack of any job description accompanied in turn by unclear authority delegation or confusion in assignment of responsibility.

Under the MBO system, the necessary first step in improving the productivity and development of an individual is to identify the key elements which describe the areas for which he or she is held accountable. This is an "individualized," not a "programmed" or mass production process. Employees should therefore write down the duties, actions, and responsibilities of their jobs as they understand them. These can then be grouped for the purpose of summary into key job duties. This will provide the basis for superior–subordinate understanding.

The 80/20 Rule

The "80/20" rule, known more formally as Pareto's Law, says that in any group of activities, a vital few account for the bulk of the benefits. In other words, a few of the activities (ten to twenty percent) are more important in achieving results than all others put together. This can be applied to almost any area of the organization. For example, eighty percent of sales are usually made by twenty percent of the sales force, eighty percent of the profit is usually made by twenty percent of the items, or eighty percent of overdue accounts are owed by twenty percent of the customers, and so on. The lesson here is that the important twenty percent should be identified and made the subject of particular management attention.

The 80/20 rule applies to a person's job as well. Eighty percent of an employee's time is usually spent on a few *key* duties that account for the major results of the job. It is therefore important that these key responsibilities and duties be identified so that particular attention can be devoted to them. The 80/20 rule will also provide a guide for homing in on the most significant areas for productivity improvement.

Defining Expected Results

The general inclination to state responsibilities in such vague terms as "generate more business," or "reduce costs," or "do a better job of design," is not acceptable in the MBO system of results management. Objectives are not abstractions. They are the action commitments by which an individual's contribution to the next higher level of goals are measured. As such they must be capable of being converted into specific targets and specific assignments. They must be measurable. They should be quantifiable wherever possible.

How to Express Objectives

Objectives can be expressed and results measured in terms of one or more of these basic yardsticks: quantity, quality, time, or dollar value. These are illustrated:

Yardstick	*Illustration*
Quantity	Sell a sales quota of six hundred.
	Produce two units per direct labor hour.
Quality[2]	Improve the technical specifications.
	Reduction of errors.
Time[3]	Complete the project in six months.
	Reduce overhead by May 15.
Dollar value	Develop a training program at a cost of $25.00 per person.
	Achieve a return on investment of ten percent.

A popular writing style for expressing obectives is illustrated in Table 6–1. It permits any combination of yardsticks to express the objective.

Using this writing style as a guide, readers may want to practice their skill at writing objectives (expected results) by rewriting the following objectives:

---

[2] Not to be confused with a qualitative objective that cannot be stated in quantitative terms. For example, "recommend a formal training program for new sales personnel or "prepare new plant layout."

[3] If the objective is stated in terms of time, the completion date should normally be within twelve months following the writing of the objective.

Table 6–1.

To	Action Verb	Results	Time	$
To	complete	redesign of plant layout	by November 30	at a cost not to exceed $1000
To	reduce	direct labor cost on assembly line #1	by the end of the quarter	to a per unit cost of $2.36
To	introduce	the new product in the western territory	during the next six months	without exceeding the sales budget
To	achieve	an accounts receivable level of forty-five days	by July 1	and improve cash flow by ten percent
To	establish	a "charge back" system in data processing	this fiscal year	where costs will not exceed commercial rates

Improve communications in the plant.

Pursue profitable business opportunities.

Improve employee morale.

Increase department communication.

Reduce overhead costs.

Do a better job of supporting the general manager.

Improve technical assistance to customers.

Reduce scrap.

Provide more training for managers.

Reduce accounts receivable.

Tighten up on credit policy.

Criteria of Acceptance for Objectives

After objectives have been set in terms of expected results, they should be tested to see if they meet each of these acceptance criteria. Failure to meet one or more may disqualify it as an acceptable objective.

Criteria	Yes	No
1. Does the objective measure results and not activities?	( )	( )
2. Is it a stretch objective?	( )	( )
3. Is it realistic in terms of attainment?	( )	( )
Does employee have control over it?	( )	( )
4. Is it suitable? Does it support the objective of the next level in the organization?	( )	( )
5. Is it measurable and verifiable?	( )	( )
6. Is feedback built-in or can it be provided?	( )	( )
7. Is it acceptable to the individual (or yourself if it is your objective)?	( )	( )

The "It Can't Be Measured" Syndrome

One of the most frequent problems with MBO is reflected in the comment: "The nature of my job defies measurement. How do you measure creativity or intangibility?" This attitude is most likely to be expressed by the design engineer, the market researcher, the planner, or any one of the many staff employees of "service" departments. The complaint is commonly found in banks, insurance companies, government, and public service organizations, and the staff departments of other business firms.

It is estimated that over seventy-two percent of the workforce in the United States is employed in service industries. This does not include those who work in "service" departments of manufacturing firms. The make-up of this workforce represents a real, but not insurmountable, problem in productivity measurement and objective setting. Work measurement, the classical technique of measuring productivity in manufacturing industries, is infrequently used in service industries and where it is used it only measures about one-third of the activities.

Managers of these activities traditionally have attempted to measure the efficiency of the operation by devising some method of cost control. This is not enough. Far more important is a measure of effectiveness. This latter measure will place the emphasis on the result.

Many of these activities are providing some service to an "internal" customer within the organization. If this is the case, it can be measured in terms of its effectiveness; the computer specialist by turnaround time, the personnel analyst in terms of how long it takes to fill an opening, the foreman in maintenance by a ratio relating his service to the user (e.g., cost per machine hour). Sometimes, the effectiveness of a service department can be measured by asking the question: "What would it cost to buy the service from an outside source?"

On dozens of occasions I have been asked this question by design engineers: "How do you measure creativity?" This is a valid question and not easy to answer. I usually reply with the suggestion that creativity in design can be measured by asking yourself two questions: "What have you contributed to the knowledge and the results in your department and to the company in the past year?" and "How many answers to design problems have you come up with during the past year?" The answers to these questions may prove embarrassing. On the other hand, if the questions were phrased in terms of next year the answers might be helpful in measuring "creativity," despite the qualitative nature of the expected results. By asking these same questions the supervisor of design engineers and other "creative" persons involved in "intangible" work will be able to distinguish between the most creative and the least creative employee in a department.

A top executive of a major insurance company, tired of hearing the "intangibility" argument and other excuses, has organized a Productivity and Performance Measurement Program. Innovative methods include activity analysis (measuring performance in field offices around fifteen activities performed), business planning (establishing standards for staff time by function within major product lines), cost-effectiveness analysis (definition of marketing/effectiveness ratios), and the allowable expense concept. These methods represent an attempt to depart from the fixed budget and focus on cost control methods of the past. It is an attempt to measure effectiveness and productivity rather than the illusion of efficiency.

Setting Objectives to Measure the Unmeasurable

Some advocates of MBO say that if you can't count it, measure it, or describe it, you probably don't know what you want and can forget it as an objective. While this may be a slight exaggeration, it does point up the need to devise some method of defining expected results.

Where the absolute measures of quantity, quality, time, and dollar value described above cannot be used, it may become necessary to invent some measure of present level of results in order to be able to estimate changes from that level. Three measures, in descending order of desirability, are: the index, the scale, and the description.

The index compares performance against some baseline level and can be expressed as a ratio, a percent, a fraction, or a batting average. Illustrations are: ratio of power cost to maintenance costs or percent of service calls.

The scale can be constructed to measure performance over time. It may be "on a scale of one to ten" or something less descriptive such as "better than–worse than" or "excellent–fair–poor."

The description is the least useful measure but is better than none at all for setting base lines for estimating expected results. "Better than the industry average" is different from "worse than the industry average" but the description can be used as an imperfect measure to state conditions as they should be and as they exist.

Measuring the Results

If the expected results have been adequately defined, measuring the actual results is not difficult. The measurement can be informal or formal.

The informal measurement is a matter of superior–subordinate face-to-face communication. Each understands the results expected and have frequent occasion during the performance cycle to achieve feedback. This is the most widespread and perhaps the most useful form of results management. Feedback is usually on a real time or a continuing basis.

Formal measurement involves the many structured reports and control systems that are used to measure performance against standards. If these systems are to be used for MBO performance measurement, it becomes necessary to evaluate them for that purpose. Is the report providing the data that will measure performance? Does it contain the necessary quantitative figures? One of the by-products of an MBO program is that the company will frequently discover that their information and reporting systems are not doing the job. They are either not being used at the grass roots level or do not provide the essential data for managing by results.

It may be useful to construct an MBO organization chart along the lines of Figure 6–5 to obtain an overall view of requirements for setting and measuring key objectives. This chart is useful for comparing existing information systems to determine whether they are adequate for the purpose of measuring expected results.

Appraisal

The process of performance appraisal was discussed in chapter 3. It is important to repeat that appraisal is the action that closes the loop in the performance improvement cycle. It provides an opportunity for superior–subordinate communication, for individual growth and development, and for setting stretch objectives for the future.

Appraisal based on the measurement of actual against expected results is a realistic means of evaluating a subordinate in terms of what counts; his or her "track record." In order for this to be done, it is necessary that expected results (objectives) be recorded on the appraisal form and that the job description be written to reflect them.

Documentation

Few people like to fill out forms and comply with detailed procedures and there is always the danger that the paperwork of any activity will become the ends rather than the means. Nevertheless, a minimum amount of documentation is necessary for the MBO program to succeed. Merely to announce that "we are going to manage by objectives" and not follow-up with some disciplined approach is not enough. A caution to remember is: "If you haven't written it out, you haven't thought it out."

The key documentation is contained in the forms shown in Figure 6–6. Each is briefly described below. The actual format and content can be designed to meet the needs of each individual organization. The purpose here is to provide the central idea.

Working Papers

Job Definition On this form employees should list their various duties and job responsibilities as they interpret them. Be brief. These duties should be grouped and boiled down until a much smaller (no more than five) list of key duties remains. Follow the 80/20 rule and concentrate on

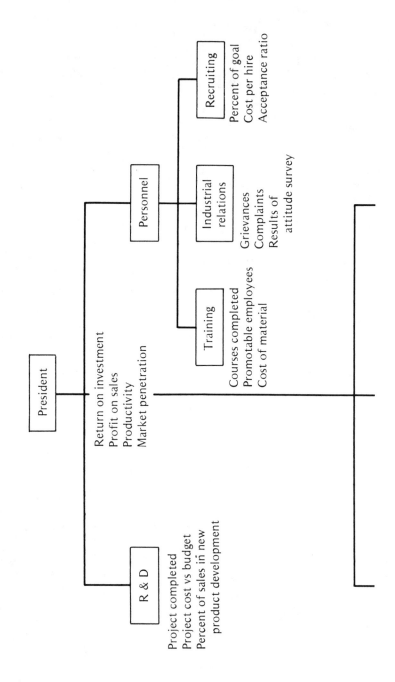

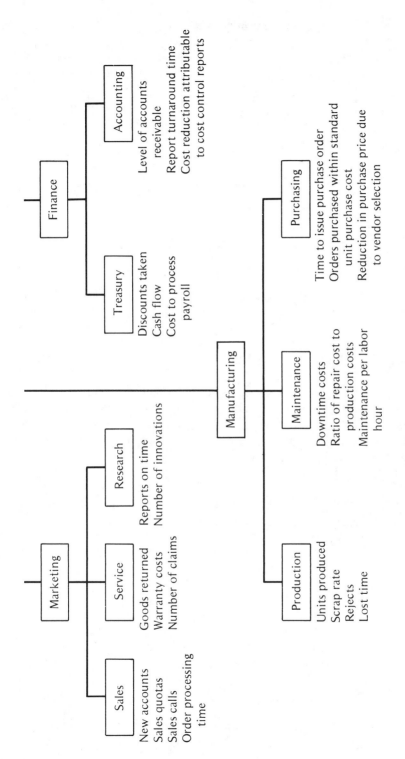

Figure 6–5. Organization Chart of Key Result Areas

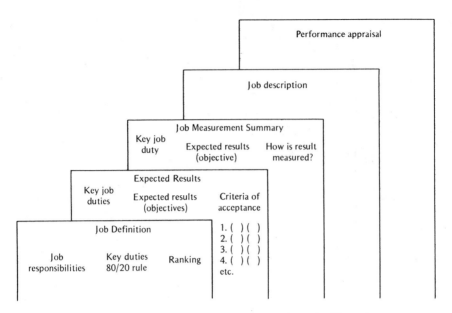

Figure 6–6.   Documentation of Individual Employee's Objectives

the few duties that represent the most important part of the job. These key duties are then weighed and ranked according to their relative importance. Any reasonable scale (e.g., 1–10) will do. This form can then be jointly reviewed by the superior–subordinate team for agreement as the basis for setting expected results.

Expected Results   In this working paper the key job duties determined in the first step are entered in rank order of their relative importance. Then for each key job duty a measure of expected result (objective) is entered. This measure is designed according to the principles outlined in this chapter. Each objective is then checked to determine whether it meets the seven criteria of acceptance discussed on page 90.

Job Measurement Summary   The purpose of this form is to summarize the source of data for measuring actual against expected results. After listing the key duties and expected results again on this form, the column labeled "How Is Result Measured" is used to describe the report (if any) used to measure the key duty, whether the data on the report can be used for measurement, whether new data may be required, or whether measurement is purely between superior and subordinate on an informal basis.

Personnel Forms   These include the job description, if used, and the performance appraisal form. Although it isn't essential to list key job duties on the job description, in almost every case the job duties and key results expected should become a part of the appraisal form.

SUMMARY: MAKING MBO WORK

It is difficult to argue against MBO as a central method of achieving productivity. The approach is both theoretically sound and valid as a practical theme of management. It has been proven in hundreds of organizations. On the other hand, it has failed to live up to expectations in hundreds of others. These failures are not due to any weakness of the system. Rather, they can be traced to the way in which the system is managed.

From these successes and failures have come a gestalt of do's and don'ts that provide a handy guide for the success or failure of the program. For those who view MBO as just another technique, rather than as a philosophy of management, the guide below will serve as a checkoff list to hasten the failure of your program. For those who sincerely want to achieve productivity through results, the list will alert you to the roadblocks ahead.

The Do's and Don'ts of MBO

The Do's of MBO

Do Design Stretch Objectives One of the most common mistakes is to design jobs so small that employees cannot grow. They become frustrated, bored, and "retire on the job." They take a passive attitude toward MBO or ignore it.

Do Be Flexible Plans and objectives are not set in concrete. Change occurs and individual results and plans must be adapted. Inflexibility encourages defensive behavior.

Do Provide Top Management Support Delegation of MBO to a staff assistant, a planner, or the Personnel Department will insure that it will be regarded as just another personnel or planning gimmick. MBO is a line responsibility. The action is at the middle management and front-line supervisor level.

Do Provide Feedback This is an absolute prerequisite to the success of the program. Feedback is not usually sufficient when provided by a formal chart of accounts or an incomprehensible reporting system. It should be achieved through feedback on individualized objectives established by each employee.

Do Tie To Compensation Although money alone is not a motivator, it does provide a yardstick of achievement and recognition. Tie compensation into the achievement of objectives, otherwise you may lapse into the practice of across-the-board compensation where everyone gets the same raise regardless of contribution.

Do Follow Up With Plans It does little good to set objectives unless people develop some form of action plan to achieve them. The plan provides the necessary organization of effort and the feedback on progress toward expected results.

Do Stress Objectives and Not The System Although the trappings of the system—the rationale, operation, forms, pitfalls—must be explained, be careful of the system becoming the end rather than the means.

Do Tie to Appraisal The same rationale applies here as it does under compensation. Job closure, ownership of results, and feedback are all essential to individual motivation. Performance appraisal is the primary vehicle through which these are provided.

Do Train The concept and operation of the MBO system is not easy. It must be "sold" and people must be trained in its execution. Original orientation is not enough. Follow-up and refresher training is needed to keep the system "pumped up."

Do Integrate and Coordinate MBO is not an isolated method or system by itself. On the contrary, it is a very fine tool for coordinating other plans and programs as well as the subsystems of the organization. MBO should support the profit plan as well as the functional plans in marketing, personnel, production, and so on.

The Don'ts of MBO

Don't Create a Papermill If employees must spend a lot of time in filling out hard to understand forms and complying with detailed procedures, you are unlikely to get support.

Don't Emphasize Techniques An emphasis on techniques, like the papermill above, sidetracks the real effort. People are hesitant to participate for fear of misunderstanding or noncompliance with a technique. Keep techniques at a minimum and emphasize that they are only a means to help achieve results.

Don't Get Caught Up in Techniques A manager who falls prey to this approach is the perfectionist who spends a disproportionate amount of time discussing, rehashing, and reworking the details of the program. This manager is more concerned with detail than content. He or she should realize that it is somewhat imperfect in terms of quantification and get on with the main idea—results.

Don't Adopt the "Busy" Syndrome Many managers devote very little time to objective setting and appraisal because they put more importance on the activities of their job than they do on getting results. They are unable to delegate. Such a manager should schedule a time for getting activities accomplished and another time for MBO.

Don't Adopt the Attitude "Do what I say, not what I do." This manager either discourages the participation with a "let's do it later" comment, or gives little time or assistance to make the system work. The result: a self-fulfilling prophecy in the department.

Don't Be a Copycat Although the experience of others may be very useful as a general guide, the system should not be a model of another organization. Avoid trying to make one plan or set of objectives fit all jobs.

Don't Implement Overnight A crash implementation throughout all levels of the company is likely to lead to confusion or disillusionment. Go slow at first. Try a "pilot" program in one division or department. Although "grass roots" or "bottom up" is the basic approach of MBO, you may want to adopt a "top down" approach for the initial implementation or until your program is more mature.

Don't Try to Quantify Every Objective An insistence on quantification where it may not be appropriate leads to "creative numbering": assigning a number to an objective because it is a requirement. This is not likely to lead to commitment on the part of the employee unless the results expected have a realistic measure.

Don't "Lay On" Objectives MBO involves upward communication. The subordinate should establish personal expected results and to "assign" them is to kill the motivation and hence the real basis of the system. Don't be the autocratic manager who determines the objectives for subordinates unilaterally and attempts to "sell" them on the idea that the objectives are theirs. Take the time to discuss the objectives that are originated by the subordinate. Take the time to get commitment.

Don't Consider MBO As A Panacea The MBO system must be supported by good managers and a good management system that includes well laid plans, an organization style and structure to carry them out, and a sound basis for control. MBO is only as good as the management system it is built upon. This is the System for Productivity Management.

ARE YOU READY FOR MBO?

	Yes	No

1. Are you *really* managing by objectives? Do you
set objectives in terms of results expected?   ( ) ( )

Are you paying "lip service" to the concept?

2. Does your objective support the next higher level
in the organization and do the objectives of your
subordinates support yours?   ( ) ( )

If no, review the concept of the hierarchy of objectives.

3. Do you use MBO as a basic tool of job development,
appraisal, subordinate development, communication,
delegation and control, leadership style?   ( ) ( )

If no, review chapters 3, 4, 5.

4. Have you defined your job and the job of your
subordinates in terms of:

Key job duties?   ( ) ( )

The 80/20 rule?   ( ) ( )

Expected results?   ( ) ( )

*If no, consider reviewing job descriptions. Also, list 3–4
basic responsibilities and match these with objectives.*

5. Can you set an objective to measure the
"unmeasurable?"   ( ) ( )

If no, use an index or a scale or a description.

6. Do your objectives meet these criteria?

Measure results and not activities?   ( ) ( )

Is it a stretch objective?   ( ) ( )

Is it realistic in terms of attainment?   ( ) ( )

Does it support the next higher level?   ( ) ( )

Is it measurable and verifiable?   ( ) ( )

Is feedback built in?   ( ) ( )

Is it acceptable to the individual?   ( ) ( )

If no, review rules for setting objectives.

7. Does your control system provide for formal as well as
informal measure of performance?   ( ) ( )

*If no, (a) establish superior–subordinate face-to-face
informal communication and (b) evaluate your formal
control system for its use in measuring MBO.*

8. Does your appraisal system incorporate MBO?   ( ) ( )

*If no, revise the system to include appraisal based on
objectives set and results achieved.*

9. Is your MBO system adequately documented?   ( ) ( )

*If no, provide job definition, expected results, and
job measurement summary.*

10. Does your program rate high when appraised
against the "do's and don'ts" of MBO?   ( ) ( )

7

Problem Definition and Analysis

What is a Problem?
The Process of Problem Definition and
    Analysis
Steps in the Problem Definition and
    Analysis Process
Problem Definition
Problem Analysis
People Problems
Problem Analysis as a Way of Managerial
    Life
Case Study: Office Systems, Inc.
Check Your Problem-Solving Readiness

There is an old Laurel and Hardy comedy routine that has been used successfully by generations of comedians and still gets a laugh today. The audience roars with delight as the comedian opens his closet door while the contents pour forth and crash around him in utter disarray and confusion.

Many managers view their job in this way. As the door to the "problems" closet is opened, out tumbles a disorganized array of crises brought on by subordinates who can't, or won't, solve problems for themselves.

How many times have you gone to your boss with the statement: "Boss, I've got a problem." And how many times have your subordinates come to you with a similar complaint? Too many times, we must admit.

There is an abundance of evidence to indicate that problem solving and crisis management take up the vast majority of the typical manager's time despite the textbook admonition that planning, organizing, and controlling should take precedence. Indeed, many theorists and practitioners define a business organization as a set of problems to be solved. This suggests that the primary role of the manager is the definition and solution of problems through the process of information gathering and analysis.

Nobody knows how much effort is wasted and how much productivity is lost due to the failure to identify and find the cause of organizational problems. We do know that if problems are not defined and the causes identified, subsequent decisions and action plans are misdirected. This can lead to large cost increases and significant losses in productivity.

WHAT IS A PROBLEM?

Stated simply, a problem exists when there is a variance between expected and actual results; between that which is (or is anticipated) and that which is desired. It is an indeterminate situation in which doubt or uncertainty is felt, and a stimulus presses for a solution.

A second characteristic of a problem is that the variance concerns you, the manager. Either your attention is called to the variance by your superior or you sense that something is wrong and that something needs to be done about it. Although managers spend much of their time in solving problems, one of their most important but frequently overlooked responsibilities is recognizing that a problem exists or is about to happen. Too often managers remain unaware of problems until a crisis is reached or affairs have gone beyond the point of no return.

From the point of view of problem definition and analysis, the subject of this chapter, we can also say that a problem exists when the cause of the variance is unknown. The essential objective of this chapter is to describe a method for problem definition and analysis that leads to the identification and verification of the *cause* of a problem. Subsequent chapters will treat the decisions and plans required for treating the cause.

THE PROCESS OF PROBLEM DEFINITION AND ANALYSIS

The central idea of problem analysis can best be explained in terms of the control process that we examined in chapter 5. It was identified as a three step process: (1) setting expected results (performance standards); (2) measuring performance against the standard; and (3) correcting the variance. The two basic ideas, a *standard* and a *variance*, provide us with a starting point; identifying the variance from standard or expectation and discovering the cause. The control process is important because it not only establishes the expectation but in many cases brings the variance to our attention in the form of a problem to be solved.

The role of problem analysis in managing work is shown in Figure 7–1. Following the establishment of expected results, subsequent control of activity may frequently uncover problems surrounding the achievement of these results or the progress of an action plan. If so, problem definition and analysis will identify the cause(s) of the problem so that the decision-making process can identify a course of action to overcome the problem or form the basis for a revised action plan. The iterative nature of the process is also indicated in Figure 7–1 which lists the steps involved. These steps form the basis of discussion for the remainder of this chapter.

The Logic of Problem Analysis

The end result of the process is to identify the cause of the variance. Until this is done, nothing can be changed, no decision can be made, no plan

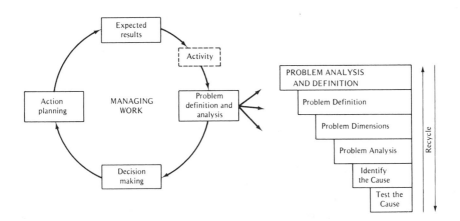

Figure 7–1. The Role and Process of Problem Definition and Analysis

devised, and no variance corrected. The process proceeds along the path of identifying the variance from expectation and then discovering the cause of the variance. For this reason we must avoid the tendency to state problems in platitudes and broad generalities (e.g., "the place is going to hell," or "we've got to reduce costs").

Problem analysis is nothing new. Its basic logic has been known for centuries and has been used in all of the sciences. One approach assumes that nothing will change or move and then asks the question: "What will happen in time?" The second approach, the one that is more appropriate to business problems, projects backward and asks: "What is it that could have been done or left undone at the time this problem first appeared that would have materially affected the present situation?" Either approach is an attempt to isolate and identify a cause and effect relationship. Both depend upon the basic logic that there is a relationship between cause and effect and this relationship can be determined by the evidence. Hence, if we can identify the event, the happening, or the effect, and trace it back to a cause, the analysis is complete.

In problem analysis, the effect to be explained or demonstrated is the variance. Since, by definition, a variance is a change from expectation, the cause of the variance is also a change of some kind. It follows logically that if the variance is to be corrected, we must know the cause and effect relationship between the variance and the change which caused it.

Figure 7–2 is a conceptual summary of the cause and effect relationship between change and variance and how these can be analyzed in order to get planned performance "back on the track." The process depicted in Figure 7–2 can be summarized:

1. Performance moves along a standard preplanned path toward expected results.

2. Due to some change, actual performance varies from preplanned performance. The result is a variance.

3. The variance is discovered and explained in terms of the change that caused it.

4. Corrective action is taken to put the preplanned performance "back on the track" by removal of the cause or the change.

In summary, problem definition and analysis is simply the identification of the cause and effect relationship producing a problem. We begin with what is known, the effect—the variance. Then, using the logical approach described here, we work backwards in order to identify the several changes that could have produced the effect. By a process of elimination we then arrive at the single change that did, in fact, produce the effect—the variance—and hence we arrive at the cause of the problem. The cause is what we are seeking.

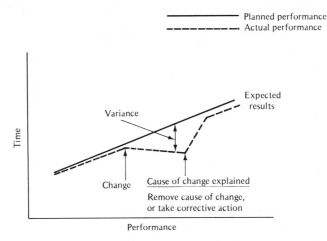

Figure 7–2. Cause and Effect Relationship in Problem Analysis

The fundamental approach can be illustrated by the yellow fever experiment that followed the Spanish–American War of 1898. It is a classic case of problem analysis.

The Yellow Fever Experiment

The Spanish–American War of 1898 ended swiftly and with remarkably few American casualties. However, by the year 1900, thousands of soldiers were dying of yellow fever. The job was to find the cause of the fever and eradicate it.

A two-pronged approach was taken to the problem. It was assumed that the disease was communicated either by person-to-person contact or through general unsanitary conditions. First, a program of microscopic research was undertaken. Autopsies were conducted on hundreds of victims. Blood, flesh, and the organs of the bodies were scrutinized microscopically in search of a clue. Clothing, linens, and personal belongings were analyzed with care in hopes of uncovering the cause of "yellow jack." All efforts were in vain.

A second approach involved a massive effort to clean up the dirt and filth of Cuba. This effort resulted in the cleanest and most sanitary Havana in history but it did not affect the climbing death rate from yellow fever. The massive fatalities increased.

Later that year Major Walter Reed, in whose name the famous Walter Reed hospital of the U.S. Army was later dedicated, was placed in charge of "the cause and prevention of yellow fever." He reasoned: "Perhaps we can't find out what causes 'yellow jack' but maybe we can find out how it is spread." The problem was redefined. In other words, if they could keep people from catching yellow fever they would be successful even though they did not know what the basic cause was.

Reed set out to test the popular belief that the disease was spread through contact with other victims. As time passed he became increasingly frustrated because the evidence proved this hypothesis wrong. First, there were nurses who tended the yellow fever victims but were no more susceptible to the disease than any other group. Second, the pattern of disease was entirely random; it was extremely rare for all members of a family to be struck at the same time. Finally, his tentative cause and effect relationship was disproven when some of the totally isolated prisoners in the guardhouse contacted the disease, despite the fact that there had been not the slightest contact with outsiders.

One Dr. Carlos Finaly of Havana, considered by many to be a crank, persisted in his theory that yellow fever was carried by mosquitoes. Despite his skepticism, Reed decided to test this possible cause of the problem. A number of volunteers, including two medical doctors, allowed themselves to be bitten by mosquitoes that had previously bitten many yellow fever victims. The results, including the death of one of the doctor volunteers, indicated there might be something in the mosquito theory. Certainly a cause and effect relationship had been established but the cause needed further testing and verification. So began the famous experiment.

Two houses were built. The first was very sanitary and was antiseptically clean. It had double-screened windows and doors that absolutely ruled out the entry of any mosquito. The volunteers in the house, each of whom had been bitten by mosquitoes that had fed on yellow fever victims, lived in spotless comfort, eating carefully prepared meals and having no contact with the outside world. In the second house lived another group of volunteers, none of whom had been bitten by mosquitoes. No mosquito was allowed entrance into this house but the volunteers lived in squalor and filth. They ate from dishes and slept in beds that were contaminated with the filth from the yellow fever wards.

The results of the experiment are now world famous. The men living in the spotless antiseptic house and who had been bitten by the mosquitoes came down with yellow fever. Those who had lived for twenty days in the squalor and filth of diseased victims, although very uncomfortable, were still healthy.

By the process of problem analysis, Dr. Walter Reed arrived at the single change that produced the effect. Moreover, he tested and verified the cause of the change. He still didn't know the cause of yellow fever but he knew the cause of its transmission. The solution then became an engineering problem of eliminating the breeding places of the Aedes Aegypti mosquito.

STEPS IN THE PROBLEM DEFINITION
AND ANALYSIS PROCESS[1]

This logical relationship between cause and effect is the central notion of the problem definition and analysis process. The steps in the process are shown in Figure 7–1 and are listed again below. These will form the basis of discussion for the remainder of this chapter.

Assuming that we have *recognized* a problem (Is there a variance? Am I concerned?), we can then proceed to identify the cause as follows:

1. Problem Definition Define the real problem and not the symptom. *State the problem* in specific terms, not generalities. *Specify the variance* in terms of who, what, where, when, and how much.

2. Problem Analysis Analyze the boundaries and specifications in order to determine the cause of the variance. *Analyze the variance* in terms of problem boundaries; what is included and excluded from the problem. *Explain the cause* of the problem in terms of distinctive changes that have occurred that will explain the cause.

3. Test the Cause Does the probable cause "square with the facts?" Does it explain the variance?

4. Verify the Cause Verify the validity of the identified cause of the problem.

The discussion of the steps in the problem definition and analysis process are illustrated by reference to the Office Systems, Inc. case at the end of the chapter.

PROBLEM DEFINITION

The most fundamental and important step in problem solving is to identify the right problem. Nothing is more futile than the right answer to the wrong question, nothing more frustrating than to spend time and effort on the wrong solution. This is why the problem definition phase of problem analysis is so important. For centuries managers have been told that

---

[1] A complete bibliography on problem solving and decision making would run to more than a hundred pages. Three sources come to mind: Charles H. Kepner and Benjamin B. Tregoe, *The Rational Manager* (New York: McGraw–Hill Book Company, 1965); Robert G. Murdick and Joel E. Ross, *Information Systems for Modern Management* (Englewood Cliffs, N.J.: Prentice-Hall, Inc., 1975); and Kenneth E. Schnelle, *Case Analysis and Business Problem Solving* (New York: McGraw–Hill Book Company, 1967). The United States Armed Forces also teach an outstanding approach to problem solving, decision making, and planning in their various staff and war colleges. Here it is known as "the commander's estimate of the situation."

they cannot solve a problem until it is defined and that a problem well-defined is a problem half-solved. This is good advice.

Most of us are guilty of the common habit of attacking the symptom rather than the real underlying problem that the symptom represents. We blame inventory turnover; the real problem could be pricing, product obsolescence, or sales training. We may see a problem in cost control and begin a cost reduction program; the real problem may be in design of the product. We conclude that communication is our problem but this is a symptom of organization structure. And so it goes. We must resist the temptation to solve the symptom rather than the real problem it represents.

There is another reason for identifying the real or primary problem. It may lie at the root of a whole tree of secondary or related problems which represent symptoms of the real cause. The temptation is to get excited about the secondary problem, or symptom, and to waste time working on a temporary crisis rather than solving the root of the entire problem cluster.

Identifying the primary problem and its cause is somewhat like a medical doctor performing a diagnosis. If the patient complains of a sore throat, a symptom, the doctor goes beyond the symptom to seek out the real cause which might be infection, excessive smoking, or influenza. This in turn may be indicative of other "cluster" problems.

In summary, if problem analysis is to find the cause and develop a cure for a variance, we must first produce a clear problem statement.

The Problem Statement

A logical problem stating process will help to make sure that the problem and the variance which caused it are stated correctly. This involves the careful identification of the three problem elements: (1) the present situation; (2) the desired situation; (3) the constraints involved in solving the problem; and (4) the criteria by which the solution will be judged.

Consider the accounts receivable problem in the Office Systems, Inc. case at the end of this chapter. Greg Peterson, the general manager, has identified a loan problem that is attributable to the level of accounts receivable and has asked the controller, Frank Jordon, to solve it. Perhaps you would like to play the role of Frank Jordon and develop a statement of the problem.

Despite the straightforward nature of the situation that exists with receivables, few managers in my experience are able to correctly state the problem on the first try. Typical problem statements include:

"Improve the collection process."

"Design a better receivables system."

"Send out invoices faster."

"Insist on faster payment or cut off credit."

"The problem is morale and communication."

"The problem is bank loans."

Problem definition can only be achieved by taking a logical step-by-step approach to arrive at a statement of the problem. This process is demonstrated below for the case of Frank Jordon in the Office Systems, Inc. case. By following such a process you avoid the waste of time that would normally occur from the identification and solution of the wrong problem, or worse yet, the symptom. Notice also that this process specifically identifies the variance.

Problem Statement

Describe the Present Situation (including identification and location of the variance)

The average level of receivables is $37.6 million.
The average collection days is 67.

Describe the Desired Situation

Reduce average level to industry average (10.8% of sales = $20.3 million).
Reduce average collection days to industry average (43 days).

Constraints (time, cost, manpower, equipment, organization, policy, customer, and so on)

Time: level must be reduced in six months.
Time: level must be reduced 5% below industry average in twelve months.
Resources: no additional personnel or equipment.

Criteria for Evaluation of Problem Solution (how will the boss judge whether problem is solved?)

Average collection time of 43 days and receivables level of $20.3 million to be achieved in six months. These levels to be improved by 5% in twelve months.

Statement of the Problem

The accounts receivable level must be reduced to $20.3 million and the average collection days to 43 in six months, and these figures must be reduced by 5% in the following six months. There can be no increase in personnel or equipment to achieve these objectives.

Notice that the problem statement process identified the variance as well as the action necessary to solve the problem. We now proceed to get more specific regarding the dimensions of the variance. We want to know its specifications more precisely.

Specify the Variance

Earlier in this chapter we said that the central theme of problem definition and analysis was the identification of the cause and effect relationship and that this relationship could be determined by evidence; a careful examination of the facts surrounding the variance we wish to explain. This process means information gathering.

It has been said that the recipe for problem solution is "90 percent information and 10 percent inspiration." This statement may be over-emphasizing the need to "get the facts," but it does point up the need for organizing the information surrounding the variance to be explained. It is necessary, therefore, to define the problem dimensions.

The admonition to "get the facts" does not mean that we should overlook opinion. Indeed, we need opinions regarding the problem in order to test them against reality. To avoid getting different opinions or asking questions is to fall into a common trap of seeking only those facts that support a conclusion that we have already reached. That is the worst possible approach to research or problem solving.

On the other hand, opinions should not be given too much weight unless they are thought out in relation to the problem at hand. "Top of the head" opinions are too frequently premature, self-serving, or representative of a parochial point of view.

Specification of the variance involves answering the traditional questions: Who? What? Where? When? How much? In other words, having identified the variance, we now proceed to describe it in such a way that subsequent analysis will allow us to trace the variance back in time to its underlying cause. Specification of the variance draws a factual picture.

In the case of Frank Jordon's accounts receivable problem in the Office Systems, Inc. case, the facts and opinions contained in his problem file would fit into the standard specification format.

PROBLEM ANALYSIS

After reviewing these problem specifications, Frank Jordon should have a fairly good picture of what kind of trouble he has. He is now ready to focus his attention on analyzing the problem by limiting it to manageable de-

Question	Specification of The Variance
Who is the person, unit, or object involved in the variance?	The bank is disallowing credit. Customer accounts are overdue. Accounts Receivable Department isn't collecting. Warehouse personnel grumbling about harrassment. Sales Department adding customers and processing orders.
What is the variance? What is wrong?	Average collection days increased from 42 to 67 days and outstanding receivables from $18 million to $37.6 million.
Where is the person, unit, or object located and where is the variance?	Overdue customers are located in all sales territories but confined largely to company items, not resale items.
When did the variance begin and what has been the pattern of the trouble?	The level of receivables started up in September and has grown steadily since that time. No irregular pattern of activity can be discerned.
How Much does the variance amount to and how many people, units, or objects are involved?	Receivables level exceeds industry standards and bank demands by 23 days and $17.3 million.

tails. He wants to eliminate the nonrelevant aspects in order to organize the pertinent facts that will help him identify the cause of the problem. He wants to get more specific by identifying the boundaries of the variance. In other words, he wants to know what is inside and outside the boundaries of the problem.

Analyze the Variance

	Variance Includes	*Variance Excludes*
Who	Primarily customers for resale items.	Few customers for company manufactured items.

What	Exceeds standard by 23 days and $17.3 million.	Above standard prior to September.
Where	All customers and all territories.	Not isolated to specific customers or territories (except as described under *who* above).
When	Started in September and increasing steadily since that time.	Not prior to September. Not isolated instances.
How Much	Majority of customers for resale items.	Not isolated complaints.

The variance now begins to take on a specific rather than a general form and the specific nature of the variance, as determined from the variance analysis above, provides us with clues as to the possible causes. These clues can be summarized:

1. The variance involves mostly resale items.

2. The variance involves all customers and territories.

3. The variance began in September and has grown steadily since that time.

The next step is to analyze these distinctions (clues) for possible changes that may lead to the cause of the problem.

Explain the Cause

After the foregoing analysis of the variance we are now ready to attempt the identification of a cause and effect relationship. This is done in two steps.

First we examine the distinctions between what is included and what is excluded from the problem boundaries. These distinctions are clues to problem cause. In the Office Systems, Inc. case, the Analyze the Variance step performed above points out two distinctions: (1) the overdue accounts receivables could be traced primarily to resale items rather than company manufactured items, and (2) the level of receivables began to increase in September and has steadily increased thereafter.

The second step in the explanation of the cause is to seek out some change that may have caused the distinctions. What is peculiar about the distinctions (resale items and September) and what changes occurred that might explain the rising level of accounts receivable?

A review of Frank Jordon's accounts receivable problem file reveals four changes that might provide clues to the two distinctions we have identified. First, there is the growing dissatisfaction of warehouse personnel as evidenced by poor morale and the "hassle" from Sales and Order Processing. This could have resulted in a number of "foul ups" that were planned or unplanned. Second, there is the addition of new customers during the past year. Possibly these new customers are not as creditworthy as the old ones. Could the trouble be traced to a third possibility; the paperwork systems in Purchasing or Accounts Receivable? The answer must be no because there is no indication of any change in these systems. Lastly, we note that in July the inventory records for resale items were moved from the warehouse to Order Entry and a "pre-posting" procedure instituted. This was done to expedite the processing of orders and to provide adequate inventory and order information to answer customer inquiries.

Summarizing, we can compare variance distinctions against changes in order to explain the cause.

Distinctions		Changes
1. Overdue customers are complaining about resale items, not company items.	*caused by*	1. Morale of warehouse personnel went down in July & August.
2. Level of receivables started going up in September and has risen steadily since that time.		2. New customers added beginning January, a year ago.
		3. Moved inventory records from warehouse to Order Entry in July.

If the steps leading up to and including problem analysis have been performed correctly, the cause should almost jump out. At this stage you are ready to state, test, and verify the problem cause. Once again, we can illustrate the process by the example of Office Systems, Inc.

State the Cause

Based on the comparison above of distinctive boundaries and changes, it can now be stated that there are three possible causes of a rising level of accounts receivable: declining morale and performance of warehouse personnel, addition of new customers, or the movement of inventory records from the warehouse to Order Entry.

In a preliminary test, to discover the most probable cause, we can rule out the warehouse personnel because the potential cause doesn't "square with the facts." The timing is wrong and customer complaints cannot be traced to any action or lack of action in warehousing. Likewise, the addition of new customers can be ruled out because the customers were added eight months prior to September when the level of accounts receivable began to rise. This leaves the third and most probable cause; the movement of inventory records. The cause can now be stated: "The cause of the increased level of accounts receivable is due to the change in inventory recording and posting procedures in July when records were moved from the warehouse to Order Entry. Subsequent clerical errors resulted in customer dissatisfaction and/or delay in payment."

This is the cause and effect relationship sequence we have been seeking.

Test the Cause

Now that the most probable cause is identified, it should be tested. Does it "square with the facts?" Does it explain the variance? To perform this test, we return to the statement of Analyze The Variance (page 113). If our most probable cause is the real cause, it will explain each item of what the variance includes and what the variance excludes. In other words, our cause must explain each effect that we have identified. The cause "moving the inventory records" does this.

Verify the Cause

This is the last step in the problem definition and analysis process. The objectives are to verify the most probable cause you have previously identified and to lead up to the next step in problem solution; removing the cause or taking corrective action.

For this step additional information is needed. The questions must be asked: "What do I have to know to test the validity of this cause?" and "What would the facts have to be to verify this cause?" The answers to these questions involve getting outside the body of knowledge already collected and providing new and independent information. You need to ask questions, get facts, and perform tests.

In the Office Systems, Inc. case Frank Jordon might ask these questions:

1. *Warehouse supervisor:* What action do you take when sales orders do not agree with inventory balances? Are customers' invoices changed to reflect actual warehouse shipments?

2. *Sales Department:* Is the order processing procedure for company manufactured items the same as for resale items?

3. *Accounts Receivable:* What reasons are given by customers for not
paying on time?

4. *Order Entry:* How long does order processing take before and after the
change in "pre-posting" procedure? What action do you take when
there are discrepancies between sales orders and shipments?

Testing a probable cause can take a number of forms. In some cases
laboratory experiments or sample runs can be made. If the variance is in
manufacturing, the production process can be changed and tested. In the
Office Systems, Inc. case, tests could be made by comparing invoices before and after the change that caused the variance or by "walking through"
a sampling of sales orders to see for yourself what goes wrong.

PEOPLE PROBLEMS

Most managers will freely admit that their "people" problems occur more
frequently and have a greater productivity concern than the hard operational problems involving "things." Although less precise than other problems, those concerning people can also be solved through the process of
problem definition and analysis. The difference is that in the operational
variance we are dealing with facts, data that are verifiable and available,
and observations that yield hard information. In problems involving
people (motivation, morale, communication, organization, assignments,
and so on), the information is "soft" and we must rely largely upon
opinions and sometimes emotions.

When using the problem definition and analysis to find the cause
of people problems, certain cautions are advisable. These take the form
of do's and don'ts:

Do	*Don't*
Address your analysis to problems over which you have some control.	Play psychiatrist.
	Jump to conclusions.
Attempt to upgrade the bad, opinionated information you get regarding the problem.	Make hasty generalizations that are colored by your own attitudes or experience.
Attempt to get hard information about the specifics of the problem.	

PROBLEM ANALYSIS AS A WAY OF MANAGERIAL LIFE

Did you ever sit down to discuss a problem with a subordinate and become frustrated because he didn't "do his homework?" Did his analysis overlook the basic facts? Was his conclusion based on opinion and speculation? Could you shoot holes in his written report? More important, did *your* boss ever have this feeling about your problem solution?

The answer to all these questions is probably yes.

Unfortunately, most of us jump to conclusions and reach out for evidence, however shaky, to support the conclusion. We don't go through the logical process of problem definition and analysis described in this chapter.

I recommend that this approach be adopted for all problem analysis, whether in oral or written form. The process will help insure that you, your subordinates, and your boss are agreed on a common ground. If your subordinates are required to use the approach, you can relax in the knowledge that he has done his homework and is using a rational method of analysis. The process provides both of you with a previously agreed upon set of rules for communication about problems. The same comment goes for you and your boss.

Never again should you have to hear, or say: "Boss, I've got a problem." Hereafter, you should hear, or say: "Boss, here is a problem and here is the cause."

Case Study

Office Systems, Inc.

"Frank, I'm glad we've got somebody like you around to clear up this mess. The company is going to go down the drain unless we get organized.

"Your first job is to do something about accounts receivable. Unless we get receivables down to the industry level by June the first we're going to lose our line of credit with the bank. Do I have to tell you what that means?"

The speaker was Greg Peterson, general manager of Office Systems, Inc., manufacturer and distributor of a line of office furniture and related furnishings. The company manufactured approximately 250 items such as desks, chairs, credenzas, bookcases, and so on and was the distributor for an additional 1450 items produced by other manufacturers. The company manufactured items were commonly referred to as "company" items and those distributed for other manufacturers were called "warehouse" items.

The majority of company items, about 85 percent, were shipped from the factory directly to the customers without going through the warehouse. Distributed items were purchased by the company purchasing agent and were shipped from the warehouse. The company organization is shown in Exhibit 7–1.

Peterson was talking to Frank Jordon, the newly-appointed controller, who had been recently hired from outside the company. After only three weeks on the job, Frank Jordon knew that something was wrong. In addition to the accounts receivable problem, several large orders had been

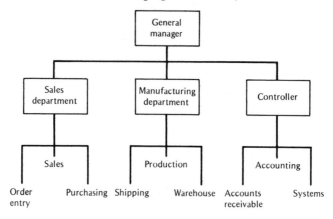

Exhibit 7–1. Organization of Office Systems, Inc.

cancelled recently because of inability to deliver on time and general confusion surrounding shipment.

Accounts receivable had been increasing at twice the rate of sales and the level of overdue accounts had reached the critical stage. The bank had recently indicated that the company's line of credit would not be renewed unless receivables were brought into line with the rest of the industry. Loss of the line of credit would seriously hamper plans for growth and damage the "good supplier" reputation that the company had carefully cultivated.

Greg Peterson continued, "Frank, today is February 1st. We've got until August 1st to get our receivables down to the industry average because that is the deadline for our credit renewal. I don't see why we couldn't beat the industry average by 5 percent in the six months following August 1st. Now Frank, I know you're new here and haven't got your feet on the ground yet but I'd like to see you meet this target without spending any additional money on people or equipment or any of that stuff."

Greg Peterson concluded: "Frank, here's the file on the problem. Everything you need to know to get started is in the file. Good luck."

After returning to his office Frank Jordon sat down and opened the file labeled *Accounts Receivable Problem.* He began to read the memorandums inside the file.

After reviewing the file, Frank Jordon began to wonder how he could define his problem and discover its cause.

INTEROFFICE MEMORANDUM

From: General Manager

To: Sales Manager
        Manufacturing Manager
        Supervisor, Accounts Receivable
        Purchasing Agent

Yesterday I received some very bad news from the First Bank and Trust Company, our bank for the past sixteen years. I quote:

Dear Mr. Peterson:

This will acknowledge your letter and supporting documents relating to your application for a continuation of your regular line of credit which has been in effect for the past sixteen years.
We regret very much to inform you that your supporting financial statements do not justify a continuation of the credit. Specifically, we note that your accounts receivable are growing at twice the rate of your sales and have reached what, in our opinion, is a dangerous level. This condition is substantiated by these statistics:

	Industry Average	Office Systems, Inc.
Sales in $ millions	174	188
Average collection days	43	67
Average accounts receivables outstanding	18.9	37.6

Gentlemen, I put it to you straight, this is one hell of a problem and we must solve it immediately. Please inform me by written memorandum immediately any information you have concerning this problem and why we are in this mess.

INTEROFFICE MEMORANDUM

From: Manufacturing Manager

To: General Manager

Subject: Level of Accounts Receivable

Regarding your memorandum, I can only say that we cannot trace any fault to production. As you know, about 85 percent of our production is shipped directly from the factory to the customer based on individual customer orders and does not go through the normal warehousing procedure. I understand that the order processing system of bookkeeping is also different. As you know, this business is built on service to the customer and we spend a lot of time expediting and putting out fires.

Since I also have the responsibility for the warehousing operation as well as shipping I asked each of these supervisors to give me their thoughts on this problem. Shipping has consistently met all scheduled dates so I don't see how the problem could be traced to that operation. You will notice in the memorandum of Pete Engels (copy attached), the warehouse supervisor, he speaks of poor morale and the "hassle" he continually gets from Order Entry and the Sales Department. Don't take this too seriously. Part of the so-called "morale" problem can be traced to the fact that for the past five weeks we have had to work all day Saturday to get the orders out. Pete and his crew are also somewhat miffed because we moved the inventory records up to Order Entry last July. This was so that the Sales Department could answer the customer inquiries and complaints without continuously calling the warehouse.

I notice that the Sales Department has added a lot of new customers over the last eight to ten months and this is causing us a number of headaches in design and delivery. Maybe that's the problem.

INTEROFFICE MEMORANDUM

January 9

From: Pete Engels, Warehouse Supervisor

To: Manufacturing Manager

Subject: Warehouse Operations

I'm not surprised that some of the customers don't pay on time. The Sales and Order Entry Departments must be really fouled up if the hassle they give us is any indication. My men are getting tired of the hassle and the overtime and if any mistakes are made you can't blame us.

We keep feeding the order entry clerks lists of items going out of stock and to be taken off backorder status. It doesn't seem to make any difference. Between purchasing and order entry we have to refigure about half of the invoices. No wonder the customers are mad. They get billed for items they don't receive and also get their bills marked "backordered" when they know we have it in stock. But what can we do? We can't control operations without the inventory records.

Incidentally, how is my request for two more warehousemen coming? We can't continue with this Saturday work.

INTEROFFICE MEMORANDUM   January 10

From: Supervisor, Accounts Receivable

To: General Manager

Subject: Accounts Receivable

As you know, our system involves three basic steps: (1) customers
are invoiced weekly, (2) past due accounts are followed up by letter
after sixty days, and (3) after ninety days, personal telephone
contacts are made.

Regarding credit checks and approval of creditworthy customers, we
send a list of past due accounts to the Sales Department monthly and
that department determines who to sell to. There has been no
significant increase or decrease of accounts for which a cut-off in
credit is recommended based on our current credit policy.

We have a lot of small accounts that probably should be written off
because the trouble and cost of collecting the money is more than
the money we collect. Going through the customer account ledger
cards each month in order to flag delinquent accounts costs us a lot
of money. Also, many of our delinquent notices should never be sent
because the payment crosses in the mail with the notice.

An additional problem is the increased correspondence and telephone
calls connected with foul-ups in customer billing. This problem has
grown considerably in the past six months. Many incidents can be
traced to errors made in the warehouse. We spend a lot of time
chasing down errors because the customers won't pay until their bill
is straight.

According to your telephone request I am providing a recapitulation
of accounts receivable over the past twelve months:

Month	Average Collection Days	Average $ Outstanding	Month	Average Collection Days	Average $ Outstanding
Jan	39	19.1	July	39	19.1
Feb	38	18.9	August	45	22.6
Mar	40	19.4	Sept	51	24.9
April	39	19.0	Oct	57	26.8
May	41	19.6	Nov	61	31.7
June	39	18.9	Dec	67	37.6

INTEROFFICE MEMORANDUM

From: Sales Manager

To: General Manager

Subject: Accounts Receivable

As soon as I got your January 7th memo I put my sales analysis clerk
on the job of trying to identify the customers who were delinquent
and why. I think we have some good clues. After talking to most
of our salesmen and a few of our bigger customers, a summary of the
problem can be stated as follows:

(1) Many of the late payments are due to the fact that customer
invoices are erroneous. Prices are wrong, items marked
"backordered" are shipped, and some items are shipped but not
ordered by the customer.
(2) There hasn't been too much trouble with shipments and
billings of company items except when the order is combined
with resale items from the warehouse.
(3) We have added a significant number of new customers
during the twelve month period ended December 31st. This is
in accordance with the annual sales plan.

The new sales plan allowed us to drop a number of "bad" customers
while increasing sales. There seems to be no pattern of customer
complaints (ie., old versus new) and in general the problem is spread
over all territories.

Aside from the slow paperwork process in Accounts Receivable that
delays the customer collection procedure, I would suggest that we look
to warehousing for the problem of customer dissatisfaction. I don't
know whether it is a problem of morale or not but that crew in the
warehouse is confused and it is causing us a lot of trouble. This
trouble increased since we moved the inventory records from the
warehouse to Order Entry six months ago. However, the "pre-
posting" procedure we instituted should improve operations and having
the records up in Order Entry enables us to respond to customer
inquiries more rapidly.

CHECK YOUR PROBLEM-SOLVING READINESS

	Yes	No
1. Is a large part of your time taken up with:		
Crisis management?	( )	( )
Solving problems for subordinates?	( )	( )
Recurring problems?	( )	( )

*If yes, you need a problem solving
methodology.*

	Yes	No
2. Do you tend to state problems in broad terms but don't define them in specifics that can be solved?	( )	( )

*If yes, follow the logical problem
definition process.*

	Yes	No
3. For your day to day problem situations can you apply these techniques of problem definition and analysis:		
Specification of the variance?	( )	( )
Analysis of the variance?	( )	( )
Explanation of the problem cause?	( )	( )
Verification of the cause?	( )	( )

*If no, review the problem definition
and analysis concepts.*

	Yes	No
4. Can you apply the problem solving process to people problems?	( )	( )
5. Can you describe the benefits of problem analysis and solving as a way of managerial life?	( )	( )

8

Decision Making

The Concept of Rational Choice
The Decision-Making Process
Decision Making and Problem Solving:
    Summary
Case Study: Office Systems, Inc.,
    (continued)
Checklist: Can You Make a Good
    Decision?

The art of management has been defined as making irrevocable decisions based on incomplete, inaccurate, and obsolete information. This tongue-in-cheek definition reflects the confusion surrounding the topic of decision making. In a survey made by *Fortune Magazine* on how executives make decisions, it was found that few of them could describe a rational approach or explain how they did it. Typical replies to the question "How do you make a decision?" included these:

"You don't know how you do it; you just do it."

"I don't think businessmen know how they make a decision, I know I don't."

"It is like asking a pro baseball player to define the swing that has always come natural to him."

One reason for the indefinite explanations of how decisions are made is because the literature and teaching on the subject generally focus on the moment of decision rather than the whole lengthy, complex process of defining and exploring the many alternatives that precede the final act of deciding. The stereotype of the finger-snapping, coin-tossing manager fades as we examine three requirements for the process of rational decision making: (1) finding occasions for making a decision; (2) finding possible courses of action; and (3) choosing among alternative courses of action.

A primary managerial skill is decision making. Many scholars and practicing managers believe that decision making and the processes leading up to it account for most of what managers do, at least in terms of their effectiveness as managers. Nothing helps or hinders the productivity of a manager more than the decisions that affect his or her area of responsibility.

Before proceeding to examine the decision making, it is useful to point out the difference between it and problem analysis. Problem analysis (chapter 7) deals with the process of discovering the cause of a problem and therefore is concerned with the cause and effect relationship of past events. We didn't have to speculate because we had access to the facts and the discovery of the problem's cause consisted of analyzing past events.

Decision making, the subject of this chapter, is quite different. We are now dealing with an estimation of the future. The analysis therefore becomes more subjective, more dependent on value judgments, and more subject to qualitative choice. Nevertheless, it is a rational process.

THE CONCEPT OF RATIONAL CHOICE

Stated simply, decision making is the selection from among alternative possible courses of action that will achieve an objective. The process is at the core of management because no plan can be developed, and no controls established without a rational decision regarding a course of action.

For managers to act rationally, they must first define or understand some goal, objective, or expected result that cannot be obtained without some positive action. Second, they must have a clear understanding of the alternative courses of action by which a goal could be reached under existing circumstances and limitations. Third, the rational decision maker must also have the skills necessary to analyze and evaluate alternatives in light of the goal sought. A final condition in rational decision making is that the alternative selected must be the one that best satisfies or optimizes goal achievement. This last requirement, optimization of goal achievement, means that some criteria must be established by which alternatives can be measured.

The process of decision making that we will examine in this chapter is an imperfect one. It is imperfect because the factors affecting the decision cannot always be quantified. Value judgments are necessary. This is as it should be. Despite the recent growth of quantitative decision-making techniques (for instance, operations research, simulation), the overwhelming number of decisions faced by the ordinary manager are a combination of qualitative factors and are therefore probabilistic in nature. They must be made under conditions of uncertainty and with imperfect information. They must be made rapidly. There are no absolutely right answers, but the rational process will provide the best answer for you in accomplishing your expected results and overcoming the causes of your problems.

The techniques of decision analysis examined in this chapter will provide a method of analysis that is systematic, that will apply to almost any decision you are required to make, and will maximize your chances of making a right decision that can be implemented with confidence.

Like problem definition and analysis (chapter 7), decision making is nothing new. It has been around a long time. Unlike problem analysis, however, decision making lacks an historical cause and effect relationship. It is basically choosing for the future. Nevertheless, both problem analysis and decision making have the same result in mind; achieving expected results. The role of both processes in managing work is shown in Figure 8–1. This figure also shows the steps in the decision-making process. These are listed below[1] and form the basis of discussion for this chapter:

Step One   *Define the Objective.* Restate the expected results sought, the cause of the problem to be solved, or the purpose of the decision.

[1] Each of the steps in the decision-making process is illustrated by the Office Systems, Inc. case at the end of this chapter.

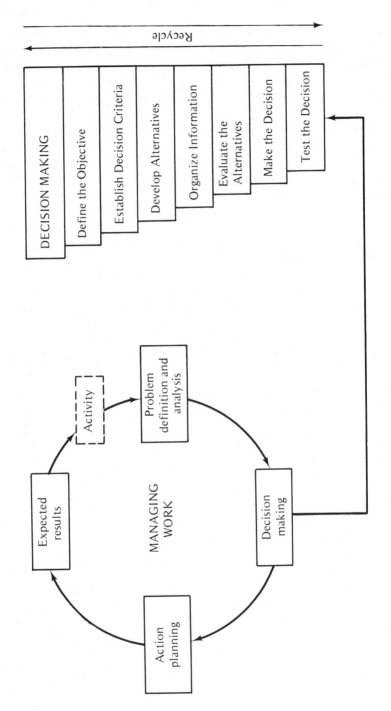

Figure 8–1. The Role and Process of Decision Making

Step Two   *Establish Decision Criteria.* Develop the factors or criteria, the yardsticks of measurement against which alternative courses of action can be weighed, one against the other.

Step Three   *Develop Alternatives.* State two or more courses of action that will achieve the objective.

Step Four   *Organize Information.* Establish the premises, the information, the "facts" surrounding the alternatives.

Step Five   *Evaluate the Alternatives.* Judge each alternative against the decision criteria in order that the optimum choice can be made.

Step Six   *Make the Decision.* Choose the best alternative.

Step Seven   *Test the Decision.* Evaluate the chosen alternative to see whether it is suitable, feasible, acceptable, and whether it is the best choice in view of potential problems.

THE DECISION-MAKING PROCESS

Step One: Define the Objective of the Decision

This first step is similar to the problem definition phase in problem analysis. Here we review the purpose of making the decision. What is it that we must decide about? What is it that must be done?

In most cases, our definition of the objective of the decision will be concerned with the question: "How do I achieve the results expected?" or "What do I do about the cause of the problem that I have identified?"

In the chapter on problem definition and analysis I warned against the tendency to rush out and solve a problem that is not first defined. The same caution applies in decision making. Nothing is more futile than a decision that solves the wrong problem or the selection of a course of action before you decide where it is you want to go.

In most cases the objective of the decision will read: "The objective of this decision is to select the best alternative for . . ." For example:

"The objective of this decision is to determine

What is the best course of action to reduce costs,

Which individual should be selected for a vacancy,

Which vendor should be given the contract,

What is the best location for a new plant,

Should we approve a coffee break,

How can I reduce direct labor costs on line #1,

What should be our new credit policy?"

and so on . . .

In the Office Systems, Inc. case at the end of this chapter, the objective of the decision might be stated: "The objective of this decision is to select the best data processing system for the company's long-term future."

Step Two: Establish Decision Criteria

If, as we have already agreed, decision making is selection from among alternatives, then it follows that criteria of selection are necessary. How is one to choose between alternatives A, B, and C unless the yardsticks of measurement are established beforehand? If there is a choice, there are two or more alternatives and there must be some measures to determine the relative values of each.

A typical decision that many of us face is the choice of a particular driving route from our homes to work each day. In choosing between two or more alternate routes we may consider such decision criteria as distance, elapsed time of travel, number of stoplights, amount of traffic, safety, comfort, gasoline consumptions, and so on. By identifying these criteria and assigning relative weights of importance to each, we can evaluate each alternative and choose the one that achieves the best overall balance.

The list of criteria for all decisions within the total organization is almost endless. Table 8-1 shows a few criteria for different problems.

Table 8-1.

Decision	Decision Criteria
Introduce new product?	Profitability
	Reputation
	Design costs
	Availability of sales training
Select new vendor	Delivery time
	Technical specifications
	Price
	Credit policy
Select plant site	Availability of labor
	Availability of transportation
	Union situation
	Willingness of personnel to move

Each decision has its own set of criteria. A good starting point is the check-off list below. It will help ensure that major criteria have been considered.

Check-off List for Major Decision Criteria

Time. How long will it take to implement the decision?

Cost. How much will this alternative cost?

Equipment. Do we have the equipment?

Materials. Are suitable materials available?

Manpower. Do we have the personnel skills available?

Customer. Will the customer be satisfied?

Competition. Can we be hurt by the competition?

Risk. Is the payoff justified by the risk?

Organizational Impact. Will the decision be accepted? What will be the impact on morale? Are we organized to implement the decision?

Return-on-Investment. What is the return on investment?

Sales. What is impact of this decision on sales?

Cash Flow. Is cash flow positive? How much? When is payoff?

Company Policy. What is the company policy regarding this proposed alternative?

Values of Management. What are the values of management regarding risk, timing, conservativeness? How will these values affect the decision?

In the Office Systems, Inc. case at the end of the chapter, the decision criteria that Frank Jordan might develop for the data processing decision are these:

Breakeven point (critical criteria)

Turnaround time (critical criteria)

Return on investment

Initial cost

Organizational impact, improved management

Supports data processing master plan

Time to implement

Design costs

Operating costs

Critical Criteria

Perhaps the most important task in decision analysis is the identification of the critical criteria. This is a factor that is critical to the attainment of the objective. To put it another way, a critical criteria is one that rules out an alternative as a course of action unless it can be overcome. If a ten percent profit is a requirement (critical criteria), all alternatives that do not achieve this rate of profit can be ruled out. There is no point in considering them. If the company is in a serious cash position and cannot raise cash for a plant expansion, then plant expansion is ruled out because of cash requirements.

It is important to identify critical criteria in the early stages of analysis so that the search for alternatives and related information can be confined to those that are realistic. Any alternative that doesn't measure up to the requirement of the critical criteria simply cannot be considered.

In the Office Systems, Inc. case, the general manager of the company has identified two critical criteria. First, he has said that no data processing system should be considered that will cost the company more money than the money it saves. In other words, the system selected must not exceed the breakeven point. Second, he stated that the system selected must provide a capability for inquiry (by both customers and in-plant personnel) during the same day the inquiry is made. If a customer wants the status of an order or if the production manager wants the work in process status, the system must be able to provide the information on the same working day. This capability is known as turnaround time. So in this decision analysis, Frank Jordan has identified two *critical criteria: breakeven point* and *turnaround time*. Any decision that is made must satisfy these two requirements.

Step Three: Develop Alternatives

Decision making is, by definition, making a choice between two or more alternatives. No alternatives means no decision. It should therefore be a universal rule that every problem to be solved, every decision to be made, should be accompanied by several alternatives. In management, as in science, we start not with the facts but with untested hypotheses; alternatives that can be tested against the decision criteria previously established.

Most of us fail to consider a full range of alternatives because we are conditioned by experience to jump to conclusions, to focus on a preconceived answer. We start out by assuming that our course of action is right and others are wrong.

Almost as bad as jumping to conclusions is the tendency to adopt an "either–or" approach that develops only two alternatives, one at both extremes of possible courses of action. Because we have been preconditioned to believe that profit is the difference between sales price and production costs, we develop only two extreme alternatives: (1) sell more, or (2) cut production costs. We don't consider the alternatives of product redesign, product mix changes, increasing prices, or subcontracting part of the manufacturing job. The old saying still applies: "There is more than one way to skin a cat."

For many decisions the alternatives are simply "go" versus "no go" or "yes, we do" versus "no, we don't." In other cases the alternatives are fixed for us. Examples of this would include the choice between two candidates for promotion, the choice between three vendors, or the choice between a limited number of pieces of equipment to do a job.

Except for these yes–no situations, or when alternatives are fixed, the development of alternatives for decision making is a very innovative process and it requires creativity and imagination. Some people create alternatives by "brainstorming."

Creative decision makers also welcome different opinions and even dissent. They know that the suppression of differing opinions is the quickest way to shut off a source of alternatives.

It should also be mentioned that one alternative course of action in most decisions can be to "do nothing." To "do something" is necessary when an opportunity will be missed or when a situation will degenerate unless something is done. On the other hand, "do nothing" might be the decision if the answer to the question "What will happen if nothing is done?" is "It will take care of itself."

In the Office Systems, Inc. case at the end of the chapter, Frank Jordon, at this stage in his decision-analysis process, was able to develop five alternatives that might possibly meet his objective of "selecting the best data processing system for the company's long-term future." He listed these:

1. *Manual system*. This was essentially a "do nothing" alternative because it involved maintaining the existing system.

2. *Outside time sharing*. This alternative provides for all data processing services to be accomplished by a time sharing service outside of the company.

3. *Mini computer*. A small computer with limited applications and vendor application packages.

4. *Large computer, vendor systems design.* Design of order processing, inventory, production control, and so on to be provided by computer manufacturer.

5. *Large computer, systems design by in-company personnel.* Same computer as alternative number 4 but with systems design by company trained personnel.

Step Four: Organize Information

I have previously cautioned that the traditional advice in decision making to "first get the facts" is wrong. To start with fact gathering is a waste of time because we don't know what facts we are seeking. We can't answer the questions:

What is the criteria of relevance of the facts?

What would the facts have to be to make this alternative tenable?

What do I have to know to test the validity of this alternative?

Of course it is impossible to ignore facts during steps one through three of the decision-making process but if decision criteria and alternatives are first established, the information-gathering phase can proceed without detours and with a much greater economy of effort because the information that is gathered is much more likely to be relevant.

What Information is Gathered?

There is no real answer to this question. To say that you gather all the information that is pertinent to the decision is obvious. To say that you gather all that is worth its cost is also obvious. To say that you reach a balance between cost and value is a truism. As a matter of practice, decision makers can't wait for all the facts. They must decide on the basis of the facts at hand or on the facts that can be obtained within the time and cost limitations of the situation. You should therefore gather information to the point at which the cost of further investigation equals the benefit which can be obtained from the additional data.

Although the below list of information categories is not exhaustive, it does provide a convenient reminder, or check-off list, to help you ensure that no major items has been overlooked. Four categories are listed:

External. Data and information concerning considerations that are outside the organization.

Internal. Data and information concerning considerations that are inside the organization.

Constraints. Factors that limit the selection of alternatives.

Assumptions. Unknown information and facts that cannot be obtained but which must be assumed or taken for granted.

External Information

Environmental.	Political and governmental considerations.
	Demographic and social trends.
	Economic trends.
	Technological environment.
	Factors of production: labor, materials, capital.
Competitive.	Industry demand.
	Firm demand.
	The competition.

Internal Information

The sales forecast.

The financial plan.

Supply factors: manpower, plant and equipment, materials.

Company organization: strategy, policies, program plans, organization.

Resources: people, money, facilities, and so on.

Constraints Those external and internal factors that restrict the value of or the selection of an alternative. Typical constraints are the lack of resources (e.g., time, technology, personnel, money, and facilities) or those imposed by the nature of the organization such as policies and procedures.

Assumptions Assumptions include those items of information that bear upon the selection of an alternative but cannot be obtained for forecast with an adequate degree of certainty. Typical assumptions are those related to resource availability, sales, levels, economic conditions, weather, level of technology, competitive environment, interest rates, and so on. Remember: *Don't assume the problem away.*

The Information Matrix

For those decisions that have a number of alternatives and decision criteria it is frequently difficult to organize the information for study and evaluation. One way to do this is to construct some type of information matrix such as the one shown in Figure 8–2. This is a convenient way to summarize what might otherwise be an unmanageable amount of information.

Note that in the Office Systems, Inc. case at the end of the chapter, Frank Jordon has constructed an information matrix to summarize the decision criteria surrounding the alternatives for meeting the objective of his data processing decision.

Information Summary

Decision Criteria	Alternative #1	Alternative #2	Alternative #3	Alternative #4
Criteria #1	Information summary			
Criteria #2		Information summary		
Criteria #3			Information summary	
Criteria #4				Information summary
Criteria #5				

Figure 8–2. Information Matrix

Step Five: Evaluate the Alternatives

At this point in the decision-making process, all the hard work has been completed. Criteria are established, alternatives developed, and information organized. It now remains to evaluate the alternatives against the criteria and information in light of the objective sought. One alternative may appear to be the most profitable but is ruled out because of the critical criteria of cash availability; another meets the return on investment criteria but involves a large degree of risk; still another better suits the customer's requirements. Which one should you choose?

The Decision Analysis Worksheet

The information needed to make a rational choice between alternatives is best organized on the Decision Analysis Worksheet (Figure 8–3). This is an excellent method for summarizing information and for bringing some quantification to what is otherwise a qualitative decision based on value judgments.

The technique is comprised of the four steps of *classifying, weighting,* and *rating* the decision criteria and then *ranking* the value of each alternative. These steps are summarized:

Step	*How it is performed*
1. *Classify* the decision criteria.	Separate into critical and regular.
2. *Weight* the decision criteria.	Assign a weight (on a scale of 1 to 10) to each criteria relative to its importance against other criteria.
3. *Rate* the alternatives.	Assign a rating (excellent, good, average, poor) to each alternative depending on how it fulfills the requirements of each criteria.
4. *Rank* the weighted and rated values of each alternative.	Extend the weighted and rated values as determined in steps 2 and 3 and arrive at a total value for each alternative.

Classify the Decision Criteria

Decision criteria have been classified as critical and regular, or non-critical. By distinguishing between these two classifications, we highlight the critical criteria, the one or more factors that must be satisfied before any alternative can be considered as a course of action. To say it another way, critical criteria represent mandatory requirements; these cannot be compromised and must be satisfied by a given alternative or it is eliminated as a viable course of action. Critical criteria must be satisfied by the alternative under consideration.

In the Office Systems, Inc. case, the critical criteria have been defined as: (1) breakeven point, and (2) turnaround time must be one day. On the Decision Analysis Worksheet we enter these critical criteria. Then, for each alternative, we ask the question: "Are the criteria satisfied by the alternative?" If the answer is no, that alternative is eliminated from further consideration. Notice on the Decision Analysis Worksheet in Figure 8–3 that two alternatives have been eliminated by this process. Alternative #4 is eliminated because the extra cost of vendor systems design pushes the total cost beyond the breakeven point. Alternative #2 is eliminated because the time sharing service from outside the company cannot meet the turnaround time requirements because of the batch processing method of data processing.

Now that the critical criteria have "been taken care of," we can proceed to the regular decision criteria. These are also shown in Figure 8–3.

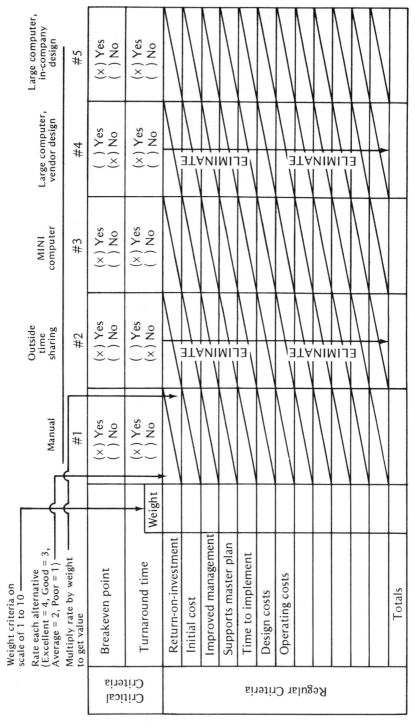

Figure 8–3. Decision Analysis Worksheet

The worksheet is organized as a matrix. Along the top are five alternatives:

	Manual #1	Outside time sharing #2	MINI computer #3	Large computer, vendor design #4	Large computer, in-company design #5
Critical Criteria					
Breakeven point	(x) Yes ( ) No	(x) Yes ( ) No	(x) Yes ( ) No	( ) Yes (x) No	(x) Yes ( ) No
Turnaround time	(x) Yes ( ) No	( ) Yes (x) No	(x) Yes ( ) No	(x) Yes ( ) No	(x) Yes ( ) No

Instructions (left side):
- Weight criteria on scale of 1 to 10
- Rate each alternative (Excellent = 4, Good = 3, Average = 2, Poor = 1)
- Multiply rate by weight to get value

Weight column applies to Regular Criteria.

Regular Criteria:
- Return-on-investment
- Initial cost
- Improved management
- Supports master plan
- Time to implement
- Design costs
- Operating costs
- Totals

Alternatives #2 (Outside time sharing) and #4 (Large computer, vendor design) are marked ELIMINATE.

Weight the Regular Decision Criteria

After eliminating any alternatives that fail to pass the "critical criteria" test, we now proceed to evaluate the remaining alternatives.

The first step is to express some sort of preference for one criteria over the others by assigning differential numerical weights. By this process we will establish the relative importance of each criteria against all other criteria. A good way to do this is to pick that criteria that is considered the most important and give it a value of ten. The remaining criteria can then be assigned weights that are relative to the "most important" criteria.

For the Office Systems, Inc. case, Frank Jordon has assigned the weights shown in Figure 8–4. Notice that he has assigned the highest or "most important" weight to improved management. He has given this a value of ten and the remaining criteria are assigned values relative to this one.

Rate the Alternatives

The last step prior to ranking and selecting the best alternative is to rate them in accordance with their effectiveness in fullfilling the requirement of the decision criteria. For this purpose you can devise your own ranking scale (e.g., 1–10) or can use the one that I recommend. A good rating system is based on this scale: Excellent (4), good (3), average (2), poor (1).

In the Office Systems, Inc. case, Frank Jordon has assigned relative ratings to the remaining alternatives as indicated on the Decision Analysis Worksheet of Figure 8–4.

Rank the Alternatives

The evaluation process at this point is simply a matter of extending the weighted and rated values of each alternative to determine the best one. By integrating the relative weights that are assigned to each decision criteria with our judgment regarding how each alternative rates in fulfilling that criteria, we arrive at the total value of each alternative.

Figure 8–5 contains the completed Decision Analysis Worksheet for the decision regarding the selection of a data processing system in the Office Systems, Inc. case. Notice that the total values for each alternative have been computed and entered on the worksheet.

Step Six: Make the Decision

The decision is now ready to be made. The objective has been stated, the criteria established, the information organized, and the alternatives evalu-

Weight criteria on scale of 1 to 10

Rate each alternative (Excellent = 4, Good = 3, Average = 2, Poor = 1)

Multiply rate by weight to get value

	Weight	Manual #1	Outside time sharing #2	MINI computer #3	Large computer, vendor design #4	Large computer, in-company design #5
Critical Criteria						
Breakeven point		(x) Yes ( ) No	(x) Yes ( ) No	(x) Yes ( ) No	( ) Yes (x) No	(x) Yes ( ) No
Turnaround time		(x) Yes ( ) No	( ) Yes (x) No	(x) Yes ( ) No	(x) Yes ( ) No	(x) Yes ( ) No
Regular Criteria						
Return-on-investment	9	2	ELIMINATE	3	ELIMINATE	4
Initial cost	7	4		4		1
Improved management	10	1		2		4
Supports master plan	6	1		2		4
Time to implement	5	4		3		2
Design costs	6	3		3		2
Operating costs	7	1		3		3
Totals						

Figure 8-4. Decision Analysis Worksheet

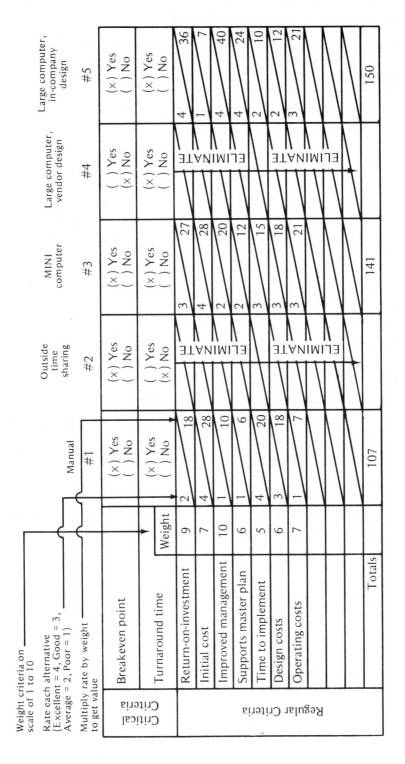

Figure 8-5. Decision Analysis Worksheet

ated. At this point the decision should "make itself." The course of action
can now be chosen from the best of three remaining and in the Office
Systems, Inc. case can be stated: "The best data processing system for the
company's long-term future is alternative #5: a large computer accompanied by systems design by in-company personnel."

Step Seven: Test the Decision

This is the last step in the decision-making process and it is performed
as a final check to make sure that we haven't overlooked any potential
problems and that the decision we have reached is the best one. The
technique for performing the test is the Decision Testing Worksheet
shown in Figure 8–6.

	Manual system Alternative #1		MINI computer Alternative #2		Large computer, in-company design Alternative #3	
Suitable: Does it achieve expected results?	(x) Yes ( ) No		(x) Yes ( ) No		(x) Yes ( ) No	
Feasible: Do we have the necessary resources?	(x) Yes ( ) No		(x) Yes ( ) No		(x) Yes ( ) No	
Acceptable: Are the results worth the cost?	(x) Yes ( ) No		(x) Yes ( ) No		(x) Yes ( ) No	
Estimate the potential problems and the adverse consequences that might occur for each alternative / Rank the *probability* (P) and *seriousness* (S) of each occurrence on a scale of 1 to 10. (Potential problems)		P | S		P | S		P | S
Summary			Decision (Retained course of action)			

Figure 8–6. Decision Testing Worksheet

Test for Suitability, Feasibility and Acceptability

The decision is *suitable* if, after implementation, the action taken will accomplish the objective to be attained. It must create an effect which is compatible in nature, completeness, and timeliness with the larger objective of which it is a part. Does it solve the problem? Does it achieve the results expected?

A decision is *feasible* if it can be carried out with the resources (money, manpower, equipment, materials, facilities) available in the face of any reasonable adverse circumstances. In order to declare that a decision is feasible, it is necessary to visualize the tasks necessary to carry it out and then determine the prospects of success.

The test for *acceptability* is really a double check on the cost–benefit analysis previously done when alternatives were weighed. It basically involves answering the question: "Are the probable results worth the costs?"

In the Office Systems, Inc. case, the three retained alternatives (alternatives #1,3,5) are put to the test (Figure 8–6) and each of them is deemed to be suitable, feasible, and acceptable.

Test for Potential Problems

Most of us have had the experience of making a decision and having it go completely wrong during or after implementation. After the autopsy we ask: "What went wrong?" and when we discover the cause of failure we say: "I never thought of that!" The purpose of the test for potential problems is to "think of that" before it happens. We want to avoid disaster before it strikes by predicting what can go wrong. All problems can't be predicted but we should do the best we can to foresee them.

This test involves the identification of potential problems and assigning some estimate of the probability of the event occurring and the seriousness if it does occur. Using a scale of 1 to 10, a value of 10 would mean a probability of practical certainty. Likewise, a scale of 1 to 10 for seriousness would mean that a value of 10 indicates a disastrous consequence if a potential problem should occur. We can readily see that if a potential problem has a value of 10 for both probability *and* seriousness it would absolutely occur and would likely rule out an alternative as a course of action.

The Decision Testing Worksheet (Figure 8–6) provides a technique for summarizing the impact of potential problems.

In the Office Systems, Inc. case, Frank Jordon wished to test his decision to "buy a large computer accompanied by systems design by in-company personnel." Figure 8–7 shows his computation and test. After

		Manual system Alternative #1		MINI computer Alternative #2		Large computer, in-company design Alternative #3	
Suitable: Does it achieve expected results?		(x) Yes ( ) No		(x) Yes ( ) No		(x) Yes ( ) No	
Feasible: Do we have the necessary resources?		(x) Yes ( ) No		(x) Yes ( ) No		(x) Yes ( ) No	
Acceptable: Are the results worth the cost?		(x) Yes ( ) No		(x) Yes ( ) No		(x) Yes ( ) No	
Potential Problems	Estimate the potential problems and the adverse consequences that might occur for each alternative		P		P		P
			S		S		S
		Continued human error in system	7 / 5	Not able to handle processing load in later phases of master plan	8 / 7	Underutilized for next 3–5 years causing very high expense	8 / (9)
	Rank the *probability* (P) and *seriousness* (S) of each occurrence on a scale of 1 to 10.	Transaction speed unable to meet turnaround demands	7 / 4	Restricts ultimate implementation of master plan	6 / 6	Unable to train and retain proper personnel	6 / 8
				Incompatible with expansion of system in later phases	3 / 8	Unable to integrate with master plan	3 / 8

Summary
Selection of Alternative #3 delayed due to high probability of low utilization and high expense.

Decision (Retained course of action)
Buy MINI computer with vendor application packages and "move up" to large computer at later date.

Figure 8–7. Decision Testing Worksheet

further analysis and thought he began to worry about the potential problem of buying a very expensive large computer and letting it go substantially unused for a 12–36 month period during which time personnel were trained and systems designed. He predicted that the real payoffs from the computer would not be realized for at least two to three years and the completion of a master plan was probably five years away. These judgments caused him to identify a potential serious problem: "Computer is underutilized for next 3–5 years causing very high expense." He assigned a seriousness of 9 to this problem and a probability of 8. This combination he estimated to be so negative in its impact that he ruled out "buy large computer" as a viable alternative and therefore as a decision.

Turning to the remaining alternatives, Jordon concluded that alternative #2, "Mini computer," would be a better decision. Although this was not the optimum decision as determined from the Decision Analysis Worksheet (Figure 8–5), he calculated that he could ultimately achieve the same result by "buying a Mini computer with vendor application packages and 'move up' to a large computer at a later date."

DECISION MAKING AND PROBLEM SOLVING: SUMMARY

In chapter 7 we argued that problem analysis should become a way of managerial life. The same argument can be made for the rational approach to decision making described in this chapter.

Both techniques, problem analysis and decision making, should become second nature for you, your subordinates, and your relations with your superiors.

If the rational problem-solving and decision-making methodologies outlined in these two chapters are followed they will provide these very important benefits:

1. People will take a rational approach to organizational problems rather than jumping to conclusions based on preconceived notions of what is right.

2. There will be a common vocabulary and approach to planning staff work that will improve communication and reduce conflict.

3. The approach will go a long way toward improving our systems approach to management which (a) focuses on results, and (b) achieves organizational integration.

Case Study

Office Systems, Inc. (continued)

It was late May and Frank Jordon, the controller of Office Systems, Inc., was relaxed and confident as he entered the office of Greg Peterson, the general manager. Jordon's confidence was due to his success in reducing the level of accounts receivable to that amount required by the bank for renewal of the company's line of credit.

Reduction of the level of accounts receivable had been a simple matter once Jordon identified the cause of the problem. He recalled how overdue accounts had risen to a dangerous level because of serious errors in posting, billing, and inventory control. These errors in turn were caused by a change in posting and record-keeping procedures involving the movement of records from Warehousing to Order Entry. Jordon smiled as he recalled how the problem solution had involved a rather simple redesign of the paperwork system.

Partly as a result of the accounts receivable problem, Jordon had decided to undertake a study that would lead to the redesign of all information systems in the company and the probable purchase of a computer for that purpose. He already had written a memorandum to Peterson regarding the study and it was this subject that accounted for his visit on this particular morning.

"Good morning, Frank," greeted Greg Peterson, the general manager. "First, let me congratulate you again on solving the receivables problem. It looks like our credit situation is fine now."

148

"Thanks again, Greg," replied Jordon. "As you know from my memorandum, this incident only serves to point up a larger problem of information systems design throughout the company. I would like to get your permission to proceed on a study that would lead to a decision regarding the long-term needs of the company. Also, If you have any particular guidelines or criteria, I would like to hear them."

"Well, Frank," Peterson began, "I certainly agree that our systems need an overhaul and it's probably time for us to get a computer. Lord knows, everyone else has one. And I agree that we shouldn't take a "band aid" approach. Let us think in terms of our long-term needs, our master plan. I've heard too many disaster stories of companies that took a patchwork approach to data processing and failed. I only have two requirements. First, we must be able to get fast response . . . turnaround time . . . from the system. When a customer calls about an order or when Production Control wants information, the system must be able to respond the same day that the information inquiry is made. Second, the system has got to break even on costs. By that I mean you should be able to come up with cost savings in inventory, personnel, and other applications that will pay for the cost of the data processing system that you install."

Peterson concluded: "Other than that, Frank, the decision is yours. Why don't you come back in a few days with your decision?"

After two weeks of fact gathering and study, Frank Jordon sat at his desk and began to review and summarize in his own mind the information he had gathered. He identified the two requirements laid down by Peterson as critical criteria and he labeled them: (1) turnaround time, and (2) break even on costs.

Jordon had identified a number of additional requirements of his own that he felt were useful in weighing one alternative against another. He listed these: return on investment, initial cost of the system, the organizational impact achieved by improved management, the requirement to ultimately achieve a master data processing plan, the time to implement the system, the costs of design, and the costs of operating the system.

Jordon had also been thinking of a number of alternative ways to achieve his objective of "selecting the best data processing system for the company's long-term future." These alternatives ranged from a "do nothing" decision involving the retention of the existing manual systems to the other extreme of buying a large computer and training his own in-company personnel to design and operate the system.

As a last step in his analysis, Frank Jordon prepared the "information matrix" shown in Exhibit 8–1. He felt that this matrix summarized the pertinent information regarding his alternatives and he was now ready to make a decision.

Decision Criteria	Keep manual system — Alternative #1	Outside time sharing — Alternative #2	MINI computer — Alternative #3	Large computer with systems design by manufacturer — Alternative #4	Large computer with systems design by in-company personnel — Alternative #5
Breakeven	No change	Vendor estimates positive	Yes	No. Probably take 5–6 years	Yes but may take 5 years
Turnaround time	OK	Cannot meet due to batch processing	Yes if located in company	Yes	Yes
Return on investment	No change	Positive due to clerical saving	Pays for itself	Can't estimate but probably negative	Positive. Best in long run
Initial cost	None	Low. Offset by clerical saving	Low	High. Bad strain on cash flow	Highest of all alternatives
Organizational impact Improved management	Poor. No improvement	Not good	Slow but long run effective	Good but takes time	Excellent. Improved management
Master plan	Nothing to advance	Does nothing	OK but requires more time	Takes too long	Excellent. Only way in long run
Time to implement	Immediate	Fast 6–12 months	Moderate 12–18 months	High 18–24 months	36–48 months for full implementation
Design costs	None	Included in total price	Low	Inclusive	Very high due to training and time involved
Operating costs	Same as existing	Included in total bid price	Moderate	High	Same as #4

Exhibit 8–1. Information Matrix

150

CHECKLIST:
CAN YOU MAKE A GOOD DECISION?

	Yes	No
1. Do you define the objective of a decision prior to beginning the decision making process?	( )	( )

The objective is to develop and choose the best alternative to achieve a result.

	Yes	No
2. Do you establish decision criteria?	( )	( )

Set criteria (yardstick) to measure the relative value of alternatives.

3. Do you develop two or more alternative courses of action for each decision?	( )	( )

Except for the simple yes-no decision, several alternatives should usually be developed.

4. Do you take a systematic approach to organizing information surrounding a decision?	( )	( )

Get the facts only after criteria and alternatives are established, then organize information around these.

5. Do you have a method for evaluating alternatives and choosing the best one?	( )	( )

Use Decision Analysis Worksheet.

6. Following the decision, do you test it?	( )	( )

Test for suitability, feasibility, and acceptability, and potential problems. Use Decision Testing Worksheet.

9

Action Planning

Top Management Planning is Not Action
     Planning
The Action Plan
Summary
Action Check for Action Planning

"Planning is the most basic of all managerial functions."

"Decisions must be actionable."

"One of the best ways to kill MBO is to have objectives but no follow-up plans."

"Unless objectives are converted into action they are only dreams."

These quotations from prominent management writers and practitioners reflect the widespread conclusion that follow-up action planning is necessary if we are to get results.

The function of planning is probably the fastest growing activity among the several jobs of the manager or the supervisor. Indeed, one can hardly read today's business literature without meeting frequent references to the growth of and the need for managerial planning.

The growth of this function is not surprising. Among the causes are the rapid rate of technological change, the growth of competition among firms and nations, the increasing complexity of the business environment, and the general difficulty of the management process.

The question also arises: why plan? The reasons are evident:

1. It helps *offset uncertainty* about the future. Although we cannot foretell the future, we can plan for uncertainty.

2. It improves the *economy of operations*. It saves money.

3. It *focuses on objectives*. Without objectives we can't plan. Without a plan we cannot achieve objectives.

4. It provides a device for *control of operations*. Planning and control must be integrated; a well-designed plan provides built-in control through performance standards.

There are six basic questions that arise in planning: where you are, where you want to go, how you want to travel, when you wish to arrive, who is going to drive, and how much you will pay for the trip. Since we have already answered many of these questions through the process of decision analysis (Chapter 8), it only remains to determine the route and schedule through the process of action planning.

At this point in this book, we are familar with all but one of the major steps in achieving productivity through results management. We have established, through the management by objectives (MBO) approach, the particular results expected (objectives) from our area of operations. We have analyzed the problem(s) surrounding the achievement of these results and completed the process of rational decision making; the selection of a specific course of action that will optimally satisfy the objective. The final, and payoff, step in this process is the design and implementation of a plan of action that will bridge the gap from where we are to where we want to go. This is the action plan.

TOP MANAGEMENT PLANNING IS NOT ACTION PLANNING

It is unfortunate but generally true that formal organizational planning, if performed at all, is almost always done by top management or by staff specialists rather than line managers whose ultimate responsibility it is to achieve results. Although line managers are sometimes asked to provide input to upper level plans, they are rarely required to develop an action plan of their own that is devoted to achieving their objective or expected result. The assumption appears to be that only top management needs to be involved in plans. Too often the output of planning staffs are either not communicated or left to gather dust in the files of the Planning Department.

Consider the many types of organizational plans developed by top management and planning staffs.[1] A sampling would include strategic plans, development plans, the numerous plans in functional areas such as marketing, manufacturing, finance, personnel, research and development, and those supporting plans that go to make up the package of the typical organization. The problem is that these plans are usually remote from the supervisor and the line manager. Rarely do they translate into meaningful plans that reflect individual objectives or expected results for those responsible for action. This is not to suggest that the many functional company plans are not required. Indeed, they are important for providing the basis for the "hierarchy of objectives" so important for coordination of individual effort at lower levels. But something more is needed. It does little good for individual managers to establish a program of expected results or objectives unless they are converted into action. What is needed is a method to convert individual objectives into action commitments for the manager or supervisor on the firing line; commitments that contain specific steps, work assignments, and responsibilities.

THE ACTION PLAN

There is an old adage in planning which says, "If you haven't written it out, you haven't thought it out." In practice this means that some practical approach is required in order to convert into system and method

---

[1] For an excellent description and comprehensive discussion of these many plans, see George Steiner, *Top Management Planning* (Toronto: Collier–Macmillan Canada, Ltd., 1969).

what has been done before by hunch and intuition. We need to substitute experience and "rule of thumb" with a logical pattern of organizing people and resources for achieving an objective.

The caution to "write it out" does not mean that a documented plan is necessarily a good one. On the contrary, we should not assume that the fruits of good planning are represented by documented, quantified, and detailed plans. It is the process that is important, not the prose, graphs, forms, or reports which it produces. Nevertheless, minimum documentation is a logical requirement. Both the process and the documentation provide for these requirements:

1. The Objective

2. The Courses of Action

3. The Action Steps

4. Coordination and Control

The Objective

The objective is what planning is all about. It is the reason for the planning process and the purpose of the action plan is to organize a course of action to achieve an objective.

A review of chapter 6 provides us with an understanding of the objective in terms of results expected. In that chapter we learned how to define and express objectives by measurable yardsticks of performance. We also developed these acceptable criteria:

	Yes	No
Does the objective measure results and not activities?	( )	( )
Is it realistic?	( )	( )
Is it suitable?	( )	( )
Is it measurable and verifiable?	( )	( )
Is it controllable by feedback?	( )	( )
Is it acceptable?	( )	( )

The first step in action planning then is to review the objective to determine to what extent it meets these criteria. The more closely it meets the criteria, the more easily it can be converted into an action plan.

Course(s) of Action

In chapter 8 we saw how the process of decision analysis resulted in the rational evaluation of alternatives and the selection of one or more courses of action to achieve the objective. At this stage in the action planning process we are ready to restate the course(s) of action in terms of the subgoals or the major work phases that are necessary for objective achievement.

It is not enough to simply state the course or the courses of action. These must also be accompanied by measurements so that a subgoal for each step and a yardstick of completion is established.

To illustrate, let us take a somewhat simple and straightforward objective that is expressed as "Improve the Parts Inventory." This objective could be reflected in courses of action and measurements as shown in Figure 9–1.

ACTION   PLAN

Objective: Improve Parts Inventory

Courses of Action	Measurement
Reduce backorders by 40%	Back order list down from 50 to 30
Reduce interim orders by 50%	Record of interim orders down from 4/month to 2/month
Reduce parts picking time by 15%	Results of time study of parts picking now and 10/1/77
Remove over-stock	Inventory records now vs 10/1/77
Increase stock space by 10%	Cubic feet of stock space open now as compared to 10/1/77

Completion Date: 10/1/77

Figure 9–1. Courses of Action

Another illustration is shown in Figure 9–2. This is an actual example of this portion of an action plan developed by the supervisor of the Engineering Design Department of a major corporation. His objective in this example was stated as: "Increase the cost efficiency of the Engineering Design Department by ten percent (10%) by December 31st." Note that in both of these examples the alternative courses of action are accompanied by a method for measuring whether or not the objective will be achieved.

ACTION   PLAN

Objective: Increase the cost efficiency of the Engineering
           Design Department by ten percent (10%) by 12/31

Courses of Action	Measurement
Reduce skill mix	Decrease ratio of technical to non-technical personnel from 0.48 to 0.42
Reduce number of personnel	Decrease population of configuration management from 26 to 19
Improve operating procedures	Shorten Engineering Change Order (ECO) processing time from average of 89 working days to 48 working days
Increase workload	Establish forecasting capability and apply company information system to all programs

Completion Date: 12/31/77

Figure 9–2.   Courses of Action

Action Steps

In most instances action planning takes the form of a project plan. A project has a discrete one time objective and is accomplished by a plan that has a beginning and an end and is comprised of organized tasks or action steps. This project approach is in contrast to plans involving functions or on-going processes such as selling, manufacturing, purchasing, and so on. The profit plan has a distinct beginning and end. The functional plan is continuous and is normally developed by top management or planning staffs.

Some action (project) plans are obviously more complex than others and require a more detailed breakdown of the action steps. For the action plan that is straightforward and less complex, a simple listing of the action steps, along with dates and expected results may suffice. For example, the action steps for the two objectives previously mentioned ("Improve Parts Inventory," and "Increase the Efficiency of the Engineering Design Department by Ten Percent (10%) by December 31") may simply be listed as illustrated in Figures 9–3 and 9–4. There is no need for a complicated process of scheduling due to the limited number of action steps involved.

ACTION   PLAN

Date_____

Objective: Improve Parts Inventory

Action Steps	When	Expected Results
Accumulate data to measure where we are now	7/1	Establish a base from which to measure progress
Review order points and parts usage	7/15	Identify overstock and locate shortages that are causing backlogs
Ship excess parts to regional warehouse and scrap obsolete parts	8/1	Clearing stock space
Rearrange and identify parts	10/1	Reduce parts picking time
Check records to measure where we are now	10/1	To see how close we are to the objective

---

Figure 9–3.   Action Steps

For more complex operations, the project or action plan can be organized around *work breakdown structure* (WBS) followed by sequence planning or *scheduling* of the action steps. Each action step of the work schedule is then assigned a date for completion.

ACTION   PLAN

Date_____

Objective: Increase the cost efficiency of the Engineering
             Design Department by ten percent (10%) by 12/31

Action Steps	When	Results Expected
Accumulate data to establish where department is now	1/31	Establish a base for measurement
Increase ratio of non-technical personnel	5/16	Ratio from 5:1 to 6:1
Establish department functional forecasting capability	6/1	Ability to assess and forecast department manpower levels and skill mix
Apply company information system to all programs	6/30	Increased workload
Increase use of technical personnel and decrease use of graduate engineers	7/31	Current Expected Tech 4 6 Engr 6 4
Revise procedures to reduce cost of operation	10/1	Reduce ECO processing time from 89 to 48 working days
Check records to measure where we are now	12/31	To determine how close we are to objective

Figure 9–4.   Action Steps

Work Breakdown Structure

The purpose of the work breakdown structure is to organize the tasks involved in the action plan into homogeneous groups for subsequent scheduling. It starts with the objective and ends with the individual detailed tasks. It is a decomposition or breakdown of the end result into the work elements of each major work package. Major categories of work involved in implementation are first defined and then each category is broken down into the tasks comprising it.

As an example of the development of a work breakdown structure, we can use the Office System, Inc. case study at the end of chapter 8. The objective was, "Install data processing system for company's long-term future." Figure 9–5 illustrates both the twelve major categories of

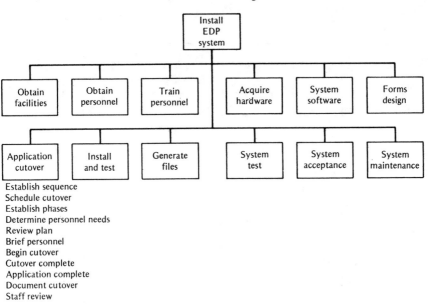

Establish sequence
Schedule cutover
Establish phases
Determine personnel needs
Review plan
Brief personnel
Begin cutover
Cutover complete
Application complete
Document cutover
Staff review

Figure 9–5. Work Breakdown Structure

work involved in the plan as well as the detailed tasks (work breakdown) under the major category entitled "Application Cutover."

Scheduling

For the simpler plans such as those shown in Figures 9–3 and 9–4, no special technique of scheduling is required because the limited number of action steps can be visualized and organized without difficulty. For a more complex plan, it may be necessary to establish a network for scheduling the work breakdown structure. A network (PERT) [2] diagram provides a scheduling technique as well as an excellent visualization of the plan of action. It depicts the sequence of tasks as well as the relationship among them. Figure 9–6 demonstrates a diagram for illustrating the task relationships for the major categories of work shown in Figure 9–5.

Coordination and Control

Plans must be coordinated and controlled, otherwise the objective will never be achieved or will be achieved at unnecessary cost or time delays.

---

[2] PERT or PERT/CPM stands for Program Evaluation Review Technique/Critical Path Method.

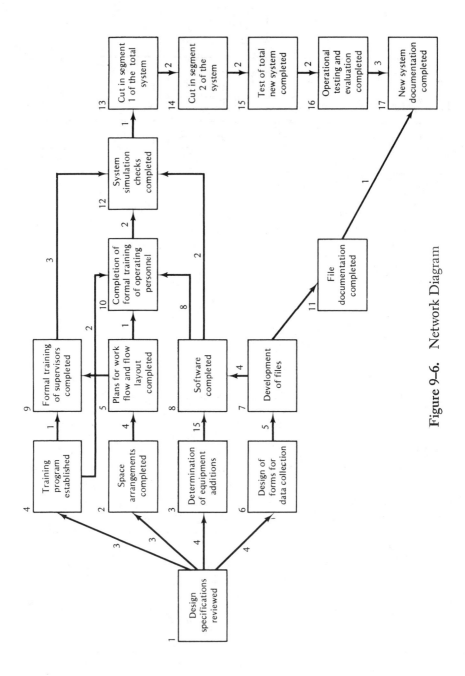

Figure 9-6. Network Diagram

162

Coordination is required both vertically and horizontally, vertically to the extent that each plan supports higher echelons and the upper level plans of which it is a part. Horizontal coordination is needed to the extent that the plans of others (e.g., sales, engineering, personnel, finance, production) are integrated. Control is necessary to insure that performance, cost, and time targets are achieved.

For the simpler plans such as the "Improve Parts Inventory" (Figure 9-3) and the "Increase Efficiency of the Engineering Design Department" (Figure 9-4), the plan document itself may be sufficient for control purposes.

If additional coordination and control are required, you can summarize the action steps onto a control timetable such as the one shown in Figure 9-7. Note that this control timetable also allows for obtaining appropriate approvals from outside the planner's own operational area, thus providing an additional measure of coordination.

Objective:			Date _____		
			Scheduled dates		
Action steps	Approval	Person responsible	Planned start	Planned complete	Actual complete
1					
2					
3					
4					
5					
6					
7					
8					
9					
10					

Figure 9-7. Control Timetable

For the more complex plan, the action may be coordinated and controlled by either an *Integrated Performance/Cost/Time Control Chart* (P/C/T Chart) or one or more *milestone* or Gannt charts. The P/C/T chart is illustrated in Figure 9-8 and the milestone charts in Figure 9-9. Both of these illustrate the Office Systems, Inc. case.

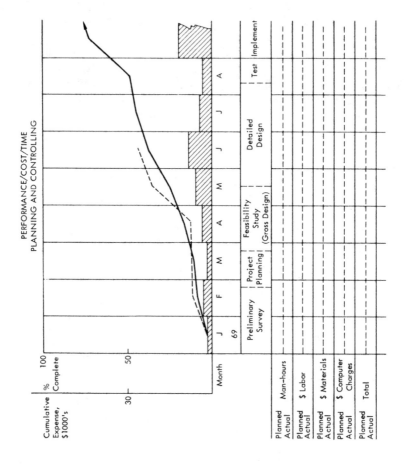

Figure 9–8. Integrated P/C/T Chart

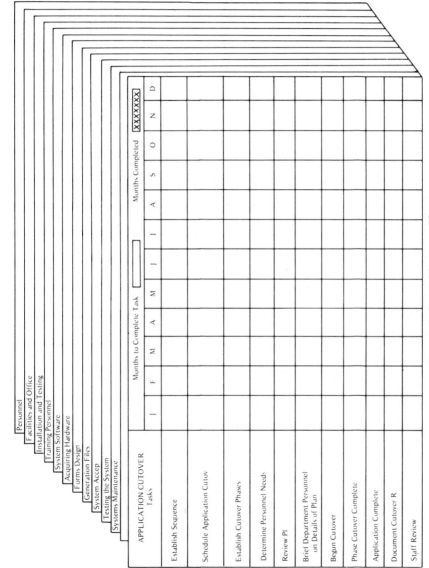

Figure 9-9. Milestone Charts

165

SUMMARY

To repeat an earlier adage, "If you haven't written it out, you haven't thought it out." Action planning requires the conversion of expected results into an actionable plan that schedules, measures, and coordinates the necessary tasks involved and provides for subsequent control.

We have examined an approach to action planning that contains these basic steps:

Objective stated in terms of results expected and meeting acceptable criteria.

Decision analysis that demonstrates a rational choice of one or more alternative courses of action to achieve the objective.

Courses of action stated in measurable terms.

Action steps that are properly sequenced and measured by the yardstick of expected results.

Coordination and control provided by an acceptable means of organizational integration and follow up.

Documentation of action plans should include the following items, depending on whether the plan is simple or complex:

Simple Plan	*Complex Plan*
Statement of Objective	Statement of Objective
Decision Analysis	Decision Analysis
Courses of Action	Courses of Action
Action Steps	Work Breakdown Structure
Control Timetable	Network Diagram
	P/C/T and/or Milestone Chart

ACTION CHECK FOR ACTION PLANNING

	Yes	No
1. Do you believe that top management plans and the functional plans of planning staffs relieve you of the need for individual planning?	( )	( )

Individual action plans are needed for results.

2. Have you converted your objectives into:		
Courses of action?	( )	( )
Measures of achievement for each course?	( )	( )

Objectives must be made operational.

| 3. Are courses of action broken down into action steps? | ( ) | ( ) |

Group tasks into a work breakdown structure.

| 4. Have you scheduled the action steps? | ( ) | ( ) |

Use project planning scheduling techniques.

| 5. Have you provided for coordination and control? | ( ) | ( ) |

Use a control timetable or P/C/T chart.

10

Managing Your Time

Needed: A Strategy for Time Management

Ten Top Time Wasters

Ten Solutions for Time Wasters

Time Management Strategy: Identify
    Time Wasters

Time Management Strategy: A Plan

Summary: Time Management Concepts

"Remember that time is money," wrote Benjamin Franklin in his *Advice to a Young Tradesman* in 1748. This advice reflected what have always been the central concerns of the Western tradition; work and idleness. The American ethic demands that time not be wasted in idleness or nonproductive work.

When the Concorde supersonic plane began its twice-daily flights from Europe to the United States in 1976, the event capped a stream of time-saving technology that began in 1876 with the invention of the alarm clock. The working world hasn't been the same since. Saving time and running out of time have become two of the major concerns of the American worker.

Paradoxically, in our technological society, time becomes one of our scarcest commodities. Unlike the underdeveloped countries, we have a limited "supply" of time. The poorest societies are those in which individuals have the most time on their hands. The lack of concern for time in these societies is expressed in the widespread attitude of "manana." Let's do it at some time in the future. Contrast this with the United States where the only manager who will admit to having sufficient time on the job is the manager who is unemployed.

Time remains the supervisor's scarcest resource. Unlike other resources, it can't be stored, put in the bank, or retrieved on demand. We can't stop the clock. Time moves on. It keeps on being used up no matter what we are doing or accomplishing. Our only hope for optimizing the use of time is to plan for it. This inexorable march reflects a paradox: no one has enough time—yet everyone has all there is. This paradox drives home the point that the problem is not lack of time. The problem is how we utilize the time we have.

The misuse and underutilization of time is a growing problem that results in part from the accelerating complexity of the manager's job. Few supervisors or managers don't frequently ask themselves, "Where did the time go?" or "How can I get more time to get my job done?" When they find themselves wishing for more of it, or wondering where it went, individual managers have a serious problem of time management. Long hours, firefighting, crisis management, frustration at working on unimportant matters, time consuming interruptions by subordinates; all of these are evidence that they either can't solve problems or haven't the time to do it.

Alan Lakein, a consultant on time management, says that most people waste in excess of 50 percent of their time despite the fact that they give the impression of being perpetually busy. It is not known what percentage of the average manager's time is wasted but it is a safe bet that it is a considerable amount.

NEEDED: A STRATEGY FOR TIME MANAGEMENT

What's the problem? We can plan and control other resources, why not time? The reason is that most people take a haphazard approach to managing their time. They try one technique or fad and drop it for a new one somewhat like the perennial dieter who is always involved with the latest diet.

What is needed is a strategy, an organized approach to the problem. In the remainder of this chapter I will provide the outline for a strategy by identifying common time wasters, suggesting solutions for overcoming these time wasters, and recommending the framework for a personal time management plan.

TEN TOP TIME WASTERS

A time waster is anything that prevents you from achieving your work objectives. Since part of a time strategy is devoted to defeating these time wasters, it is important that each individual identify those that most often stand in the way of optimizing their time. Major time wasters may vary for each manager but generally the individual's problems can be traced to a combination of those discussed below. Although these top ten are exhaustive, you can relate most of them to your on-the-job situation.

People Interruptions

All of us have had the frequent experience of being interrupted by people. Our chain of thought is destroyed and valuable time is consumed. A return to the pre-interruption activity requires reorientation and occasionally abandonment of the task until a later time. Many of the visitors want to engage in unproductive socializing. Others involve minor service decisions or administrative trivia. Most involve subordinates who are "checking back" for instructions or getting clarification of a communication that is unclear.

Telephone Interruptions

This timewaster is near the top of everyone's list. The effect is the same as the people interruption. Despite the fact that the telephone is one of the greatest time-saving devices ever invented, it usually serves the opposite purpose. Most of us fail to ask, "Is this call necessary?" We make or receive the call anyway. We take incoming calls either because we don't want to offend the caller or we want to give the impression of being available. Many calls are not brought to a successful conclusion and require subsequent callbacks to provide or obtain additional information or to make a final decision. "Let me call you back on that" is a frequent termination of a telephone call.

Doing the Work of Subordinates

Many managers are running out of time while their subordinates are running out of work. This is because the boss either cannot "let go" or voluntarily or inadvertently agrees to take on the problems of a subordinate. Upon hearing the familiar greeting, "Boss, we've got a problem," the manager feels like a reply is necessary, even though he or she is rushed or lacks complete information. A common reply is, "Let me think about it and I will let you know later." What has happened in this familiar scene? The ball, formerly in the court of the subordinate, is now firmly in the court of the boss. The time of the boss is now being controlled by the subordinate rather than the other way around. The manager is doing the work of the subordinate rather than insisting that the subordinate submit recommendations, not problems.

Meetings

Too many meetings is not only a top time waster but a sure sign of malorganization as well. When a manager spends one quarter of his or her time in meetings, something is wrong. It means that decision and relations structures don't exist or aren't working. Even if meetings are justifiable, the human dynamics are so complex as to make them poor devices for getting any work done. This is especially true for the meeting that is poorly organized, that is allowed to drag on, and to which the participants come ill-prepared. Strange as it may sound, a significant percentage of meetings are held for the purpose of finding out whether there should be a meeting. The rule is to attend only important meetings and to go prepared. Reduce the number and make them more productive.

The Stacked Desk

The cluttered desk is a very common sight in today's corporate office. Unfortunately, many managers let their desk get piled high with papers because they believe it gives the impression that they are busy. People look in and say, "This person must really be busy." Other managers justify the clutter based on the argument that it represents a method of organizing and "prioritizing" their work into neat piles. While there may be some justification for this particular filing method, consider the disadvantages to the stacked desk: (a) it allows you to delay action indefinitely by building up a backlog of pending items; (b) it's hard to find the specific material required at any given time; (c) you lose control of your priorities and action items; (d) the omnipresent desk arrangement constantly takes your attention away from doing anything else; and (e) the discouraging sight of the desk each morning is anything but conducive to getting down to work.

The take-home briefcase is an adjunct. It is the portable cluttered desk. For many managers it becomes a security blanket. Others take home two briefcases in an effort to appear twice as important.

To some managers the briefcase becomes a fine tool of procrastination and time wasting. One survey estimated that 80 percent of managers take briefcases home at night but only 15 percent open them. These people need time management, not more time.

Firefighting

This is the principle known as the "tyranny of the urgent," frequently called the busy-busy syndrome. We engage in firefighting rather than fire prevention. Optimizing time requires that we distinguish between the *urgent* and the *important*. The urgent tasks, although not significant, call for instant action and tend to make us forget the important ones. We respond unwittingly to the endless pressures of the moment, the procedural requirements of the system and the administrative minutiae, never getting around to what really counts. I have made the point again and again that productivity requires a focus on results rather than activity. We need to think of doing the right thing rather than doing things right. To do otherwise is to permit firefighting to become our objective. The conclusion is that unless the urgent task is important, delegate it or put it on the back burner in favor of the important job.

Spending Too Much Time on Unimportant Tasks

This time waster is similar to firefighting but different in that we fail to distinguish the important job from the unimportant. We don't assign priorities and hence do not allocate time to where it will do the most good. Even though our efforts may be efficient, they are not effective because they are directed to the wrong tasks, at the wrong time, or without the desired results. These activities are somewhat like impulse buying in the supermarket. If we allow our impulses and spur-of-the-moment decisions to rule, we run out of money and time before the real purpose of shopping is achieved. Effectiveness means doing the right job right.

Procrastination

Webster's Dictionary defines procrastination: "To put off doing something until a future time." Most of us exhibit this tendency at one time or another. With some of us, it's an occupational hazard.

To procrastinate is human. We postpone the unpleasant and this means doing first what we like to do rather than what we find to be difficult. Research has shown that action on 80 percent of the items in the typical manager's in basket could be completed without further delay upon first examination. Yet we usually will find a considerable backlog of action items in the *pending* basket or on a *stacked desk* because of the occupant's tendency to postpone the unpleasant. It is much easier to read the paper, take a coffee break, or socialize with a colleague.

Waiting on Others

Most of us spend entirely too much time waiting on other people; for the boss, for colleagues, for a secretary, for subordinates, for a customer. We wait for the boss to ask what to do rather than taking the initiative ourselves. We make periodic trips to the offices of colleagues in order to "coordinate" a decision and find them out of the office, on vacation, or unavailable. We wait for subordinates in order to "check this" or "follow-up" on that, efforts that could have been avoided by simple planning and control. We wait for the secretary to find a file, place a call, address an envelope, or perform some other service that could be performed more quickly by ourselves. It seems that we are always waiting on others.

Lack of Objectives, Priorities, and Deadlines

This is the biggest time waster of all and one that must be overcome if time is to be managed properly. There's an old saying in planning; "If you don't know where you're going, all roads lead there." By failing to establish objectives and plans, you are planning to fail. Activity becomes random and misdirected. Unless priorities are established you run the risk of firefighting and spending your time in efforts that are unrelated to the real objective of the job. Deadlines are necessary to insure that tasks are completed.

The establishment of objectives, priorities, and deadlines is what time management is all about.

TEN SOLUTIONS FOR TIME WASTERS

Ten basic approaches to the problem of avoiding time wasters are discussed below. These are not techniques or gimmicks but fundamental approaches to the way you perform your job. Time management should become a philosophy, a way of managerial life.

Learn to Delegate

One well-known executive complained, "Ninety-five percent of the stuff on my desk is problems that others haven't solved." This comment reflects a classic difficulty of managers everywhere and yet, of all the solutions to time wasting and wheelspinning, delegation heads the list as an effective, immediately available means of gaining more time.

Notwithstanding the critical importance of delegating and the immediacy with which it can be implemented, managers find it psychologically difficult to practice it. Most failures occur not because the manager doesn't understand the benefits but because of inability or unwillingness to apply it in practice. The manager just doesn't want to "let go." Personal attitudes need to be changed to realize that delegation is an art. The art of delegation requires:

Receptiveness to other people's ideas.

Willingness to let others make small mistakes as the price of personal development.

Willingness to trust subordinates. They will repay this trust manyfold.

Willingness to delegate by results expected.

Willingness to let go and release the right to make decisions to subordinates.

Incidentally, for the typical manager, the most productive "delegatee" is usually the secretary. It's amazing how these paragons of efficiency can, if encouraged, perform a significant number of tasks that otherwise keep the boss involved in busy-busy work.

Stop Doing the Work of Subordinates

The effective manager insists that subordinates do their own work and solve their own problems. Before a manager can delegate and develop initiative in subordinates, they must have an opportunity to display initiative. But they can't if the manager takes the opportunity away by performing the subordinate's job.

Some managers never recover from their first promotion to a supervisory job. Upon being promoted they find the new job somewhat more difficult and demanding than performing the technical tasks to which they are accustomed. They are familiar with the old job so they spend time at the technical aspects of the old job doing the work of the subordinate rather than the managerial tasks of the new job.

All managers are familiar with the greeting, "Boss, we've got a problem." Indeed, the behavior of most managers encourages their subordinates to buck pass the problem up the line. To the complaint of subordinates that "We've got a problem," he usually replies, "OK, send me a memo," or "let's get together and talk about it," or "let me know how I can help." In each case the manager has taken the problem from the subordinate. The subordinate is now *supervising the boss*. The manager wonders who is working for whom.

Instead of voluntarily or inadvertently accepting problems, managers should explain that they are willing to work jointly on a solution (by appointment) but the next move is up to the subordinate. They should explain to the subordinate: "If I accept your problem, then you no longer have one and I cannot help a person who hasn't got a problem."

Doing the work of others not only results in wheelspinning for you, it deprives them of the opportunity to grow by taking on tough tasks and learning how to perform them successfully.

Delegate! Give subordinates an assignment that is measured in terms of results. Give them the tools and the authority to do the job in their own way and get periodic feedback. This approach will allow you to dig out from under *operating* work and do more *creative* work.

Identify What's Important: The 80/20 Rule

Surveys on how supervisors spend their time have shown that much of it is wasted on the unimportant, the trivia, the activities and procedures related to the system, rather than results. This reflects a human tendency to respond to the urgent (however unimportant) rather than take care of the important. Yet we can't focus on the important items unless they are identified.

There is an old rule of management called the "80/20 rule." It applies to almost anything we do. Eighty percent of sales are made by 20 percent of the salesmen. Eighty percent of telephone calls are made by 20 percent of the callers. Eighty percent of the TV time is devoted to watching 20 percent of the programs most popular with the family. And so on.

What the rule says is: *If all the things you need to do on the job are weighted according to importance, 80 percent of the results will come from only 20 percent of the items.*

The message is clear. Identify those few items (20 percent) that provide 80 percent of the importance of your job. Focus on them and not the many urgent distractions that don't yield results. Give them your attention and work on them first. Chances are you would do no real harm if you skip the remaining 80 percent of the items that give you 20 percent of your results.

Prioritize and Set Deadlines

Now that the 80/20 rule has helped you focus on the important part of the job, you are on your way to working smarter, not harder. The next step is to assign priorities to what needs to be done and set deadlines. Both short-run and longer range tasks should be assigned priorities: A for the most important, B for less important, and C for the lowest priority. The A items demand your full attention. The chances are good that the B items can wait or be delegated to subordinates. The C items will frequently solve themselves or be forgotten if no action is taken. This is in accordance with the "principle of calculated neglect" which says that some problems will go away if left alone.

Unless you can establish criteria of your own (e.g., what the boss wants done), you might want to try these suggested criteria for assigning priorities to your work:

Does it relate directly to my job objectives?

What is the immediacy?

Who has a claim on completion of the job?

What is the nature of the work?

Can it be combined with another job?

Can it be delegated?

Deadlines for completion need to be set or the job will invariably involve a time overrun. Not only should deadlines be set but they must be realistic. Setting unrealistic deadlines gets us into the habit of ignoring them or constantly failing to meet them.

Program Recurring Operations and Decisions

One of the most overlooked opportunities for saving time is the potential for programming or routinization of simple or repetitive operations and decisions.

In one large company, well over 90 percent of the decisions that managers had to make over a five-year period were found to be "typical" and fell into a small number of categories. Despite the potential for programming these decisions, the majority of them either "went looking for a home" or were bucked up to a much higher level than was necessary.

We have achieved amazing productivity increases from automating mechanical operations but we have hardly begun to apply the notion of automating or programming decisions and repetitive administrative operations. The challenge is to move the frontiers from the simple operation (payroll, account payable, inventory reporting) to the more complex. The more a repetitive operation can be procedurized, the more it can be accomplished by a clerk, or better yet, a computer.

The work of the manager can be classified as either routine or creative. Let's give ourselves more time for the creative job by programming the routine decisions and operations.

Run on Time

Benjamin Franklin's admonition that "time is money" was nowhere more evident than among the railroads of the 19th century. Indeed, the railroad gets the credit (or blame, depending on your view) for transforming time in America. The heart of the railway system was the timetable, the matrix of system cordination. Even a one minute delay would mean that one of two trains would be a mile away from a siding or a passing track when they were scheduled to pass. Time was exact. Everyone had to carry a fine timepiece that would not gain or lose more than 40 seconds in two weeks. Watches were inspected by a railroad watch inspector.

Have you noticed the odd times on a railroad or airline timetable—10:03; 12:18; 6:37? These timetables contain two lessons. First, we must learn to block out our schedule in more precise time allocations. Avoid the tendency to assign 15-minute or 30-minute blocks just because these are round numbers. Of course, it goes without saying that we should adhere to the schedule or everyone else in the system (boss, subordinate, colleague, visitor, client) is off schedule due to the "multiplier" effect of our own actions.

A second lesson from the timetable is that we should set "odd" times for appointments. Don't say, "I'll see you at ten o'clock." This is interpreted as meaning anytime from 9:45 to 10:15. However, if you set the time at 10:05, who would dare be late or overstay the appointment time?

Do Unpleasant Things First

Einstein's theory says that time is relative. Two minutes sitting on a hot stove is relatively longer than the same two minutes spent in an activity that we enjoy. This theory explains why we do the pleasant things first.

Research has shown that the most successful sales representatives cultivate the habit of doing the unpleasant things. Once they become habit, they no longer are perceived as unpleasant.

Most of us begin the day by working on petty chores with the idea of working up to bigger projects as the day progresses. It never happens. The outboard motor catalogue or trade magazine becomes more interesting than the unpleasant items in the in basket. As the day moves on, things get worse instead of better as we realize that time is getting shorter and the priority "A" projects remain undone.

How much better it is to start with the difficult tasks. This not only has the advantage of directing efforts to where they count but we are building in a reward for having completed the important tasks. When the task is finished, we can give ourselves some time off or relax with the pleasant items of work.

Don't Procrastinate: Do It Now

Let's face it. Decision making is hard work. It gives us mental fatigue. We tend to put it off.

Most of us, having been pressed for a decision at home or on the job, have replied, "I'll let you know later," or "check back with me on Thursday." The chances are good that you will be no smarter or have no better facts on Thursday than you do today. The shortest route between two points is a straight line so don't take a detour. Do it now!

It isn't hard to rationalize delaying a decision. We need more detail. It should be referred to a committee. We need to look it up in a book. Some managers take refuge in the bottle or simply put on their hat and go home.

The conclusion: Do it now! Do it now and save the time of agonizing over not having made the decision. Moreover, if the decision is wrong, you have earned yourself extra healing time or time to correct the damage.

Have a Hideaway

A growing custom is the hideaway or the "quiet hour." Managers are discovering that the only way to avoid interruptions is to get away for a reasonable predetermined amount of time each day or week. This can be at home, at another "secret" office, or behind the locked doors of your own office. The idea is to avoid disturbances or interruptions by people or the telephone.

Some companies provide these "hideaway" offices either on or off the company premises. It is increasingly realized that an hour of concentrated, uninterrupted work can result in as much output as four or five hours of a normal work day.

Maintain Perspective

A manager must relate today's actions to tomorrow's goals, otherwise the future will be neglected in favor of today's crisis. Today's urgent activity may be tomorrow's "nothing."

The manager should constantly ask, "How does today's task relate to tomorrow's objective or the long run objectives of my job? If it doesn't relate, forget it or relegate it to the pile of priority "C" work.

TIME MANAGEMENT STRATEGY: IDENTIFY TIME WASTERS

Before developing a plan for time management it is first necessary to analyze the use of your time; to find out where your time is going, whether you are spending it on high priority activity, and the frequency and type of interruptions. For this purpose it is essential that some form of detailed time log or diary be kept for a minimum of eight to ten working days.

Figure 10–1 demonstrates a suggested format for keeping a time diary that will form the basis for further analysis. Each activity and interruption should be noted along with the time involved. It should be noted whether the activity was planned or whether it arose as a result of an interruption. This will allow an analysis of "planned vs. interruptions" and will permit a subsequent plan for interruption control. Priority of each activity can also be checked to see whether too much time is being spent on priority "B" or "C" type jobs. An analysis of the "involved with" column will tell you whether your activities are under your control or if they are initiated by other sources. If you find that you frequently work on tasks that are initiated by interruptions or the arrival of correspondence, or that you are spending most of your time with one or two people, you may have isolated one or more important time wasters.

At the bottom of the Daily Time Diary in Figure 10–1 is space for summarizing the major time wasters for the day and for writing in a possible solution.

After analyzing eight or ten working days, a pattern of time wasting should emerge that will form the basis of a time management plan.

TIME MANAGEMENT STRATEGY: A PLAN

The problem is never the lack of time . . . nobody is going to get more than what is available. The problem is putting time where it counts. This requires self-dicipline that results in a plan.

Date _____

Time	Activity	Planned	Interrupt	Priority	Involved with	Comment

Time	Activity	Planned	Interrupt	Priority	Involved with	Comment

Time wasters — Cause	Solution

Figure 10–1. Daily Time Diary

The "principle of visibility" says that you can't remember what you can't see. Nor have you thought out a plan until you have written it out. Most of us are aware of these truisms so at various times we resolve to "get organized." We make a list of things to do. The trouble is that we rarely get around to completing the jobs on the list because we work on the easy items first and never get to the hard ones. Moreover, the list seems to grow longer and faster than we can complete the items. So we usually abandon the list or throw it away and start over.

In order for the "principle of visibility" to work for time management, we need a plan that relates to our job objectives, that sets priorities for the action involved, and that establishes deadlines for completion.

Following the time waster analysis of Figure 10–1, we should now take a broad view of time by planning total time requirements for about a month ahead. Figure 10–2 is a suggested approach to accomplish this. The top part of this form provides the breakdown of what, in your opinion, constitutes an ideal work day. This will vary from day to day, of course, but the purpose here is to provide a general guide to productive daily activity and avoid slipping back into old time wasting habits.

The bottom half of Figure 10–2 is designed to set out total time requirements for a month ahead.

After establishing the broad picture, you can now prepare a daily time plan that is based on objectives, priority of action, and deadlines. This daily plan can be maintained in a desk diary or other convenient format. Figure 10–3 is a suggested daily time plan. It not only provides for planning the

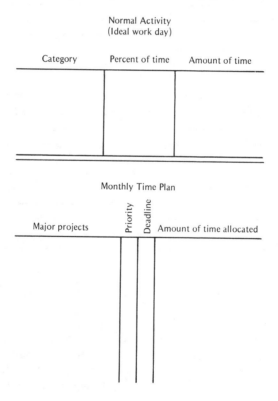

Figure 10–2.   Daily/Monthly Time Breakdown

Date_____

Objectives: (1)_____ (2)_____

(3)_____ (4)_____

Time	Project/Action	Priority deadline	Comment[1]

[1] This space can be used for further description of action items and periodic analysis of such comments as: Delegate to secretary, Get interdepartmental approval, Don't accept responsibility in the future, Consolidate with other jobs, and so on.

Figure 10–3. Daily Time Plan

action necessary to achieve results but permits a continuing analysis of time wasters as well.

The best time to construct the daily time plan is the last five to ten minutes of the work day preceding. This is the most knowledgeable time to plan your schedule for the following morning and to set your priorities for the forthcoming day.

SUMMARY: TIME MANAGEMENT CONCEPTS

Some key concepts of time management are summarized below. Many of these have been discussed above. This summary will provide a convenient check off list or reminder for the manager who is serious about managing time.

Alternatives. Decisions can be reached more quickly and time saved if viable alternative courses of action can be developed in the early stage of the decision-making process.

Analysis. The determination of significant time wasters is necessary to form the basis of a time management plan. For this purpose it is desirable to analyze the existing use of time by means of some form of daily time dairy.

Big Problems. Major problems and decisions should be allocated sufficient blocks of time to bring the job to a successful conclusion. Interruptions should be avoided.

Brevity. Economize on words in speaking and writing. It saves time and promotes better communication.

Can't Say No. Managers who can't say no to the boss, to subordinates, to colleagues, will find themselves working for others more than for themselves.

Communication. Lack of communication is a top time waster. Learn to communicate based on results expected.

Consolidation. Activities that are similar should be grouped for economy of handling. Group phone calls, letter writing, and discussions with the boss are examples.

Deadlines. These must be realistically set or we will form the habit of ignoring them.

Delegate. The first principle of time saving and good management. Overcome the reluctance to "let go."

Do it Now. Indecision and procrastination will not improve the quality of the decision or the effectiveness of the action.

Effectiveness vs Efficiency. Stop worrying about doing the job right (efficiency) and concentrate on doing the right thing (effectiveness).

Eighty/Twenty (80/20) Rule. If all the things you need to do on the job are weighted according to importance, 80 percent of the results will come from only 20 percent of the items.

Exception Management. Don't worry about the details of normal operations. Put your attention on the exception and design control reports to highlight the exception.

Feedback. Periodic feedback on progress against planned results is necessary both for action planning and control and for the revision of plans as required.

Firefighting. Crisis management. Avoid firefighting and concentrate on fire prevention. Remember that the urgent activity is not usually the important activity.

Flexibility. Some events are beyond your ability to forecast and plan so be prepared to be flexible in the scheduling and execution of your time.

Focus on Results. A basic tenet of the systems approach and management by results. Don't be a bureaucrat and get bogged down in activity without asking what results the activity is supposed to achieve.

Foresight. "An ounce of prevention is worth a pound of cure." Try to anticipate problems before they occur. This will save a lot of time in problem solving.

Important Things First. Work on the important results-producing activities first before the lower priority jobs. Avoid the natural inclination to do the pleasant task and leave the unpleasant for later.

Interruption Control. Interruptions are the number one time waster. It is essential that we get control of them or they will control us.

Limited Response. Sometimes called "the principle of calculated neglect." If items of minor importance are neglected, the need for activity concerning them frequently goes away.

Meetings. If one fourth of your time is being spent in meetings you need to get organized. Avoid meetings unless they are important and prepare for those that you do attend.

Objectives. In order for time management to be meaningful it is essential that you understand and reconcile your own personal objectives, your job objectives, and the objectives of the organization.

One Thing at a Time. Concentrate your efforts on one thing at a time.

Paperwork. Handle paperwork only once and generate as little as possible. Throw away nonessential papers as soon as you've read them. Cut the flow to your in basket.

Parkinson's Law. Work expands to fill the time available.

Personal Goals. Set goals and priorities in your personal life. Go after them.

Perspective. Keep the perspective on your daily activities by asking how they support long range objectives.

Prime Time. Find out when you do your best work and concentrate best. Take care of important matters during this time and less important matters outside of prime time when your efficiency is not as high.

Prioritize. Assign priorities to your jobs, otherwise you will find yourself working on the easy or the unimportant.

Problem Analysis. Don't waste a lot of time attacking the symptom of a problem. Go after the cause.

Program. Routinize or procedurize repetitive operations and decisions.

Reports. Cut down on them. Eliminate the unused and the unnecessary.

Run On Time. Make a timetable and stick to it. Make appointments at odd times to emphasize the need for adhering to a schedule.

Secretary. Delegate to your secretary, probably your number one time saver.

Team. Form your subordinates into a team with specific goals. Allow them the freedom of problem solving and method improvement. This will get a lot more done in a lot less time.

Time Estimate. Impose accurate time estimates on jobs and adhere to them. Otherwise procrastination and indecision will result.

Unpleasant Tasks. Do them first or you will never get around to them.

Make a habit of doing the unpleasant. Work on the difficult jobs during prime time.

Visibility. We forget what we can't see. Make your time plan visible. If you haven't written it out, you haven't thought it out.

Waiting Time. Cut down on the amount of time you spend waiting on others. If unavoidable, put the waiting time to use.

Write Less. Use phone calls or memos rather than letters. Reply to letters with a handwritten note on the original.

Index

A

Action planning, 20, 153–67
American Management Associations, 3, 5, 87
Appraisal, 20, 34–40, 93

B

Behavioral model, 73–74
Blake, Robert, 65
Bureaucratic structure, 73
Bureaucracy, 15–16

C

Cascade effect, 82–83
Closure, 31, 33
Communication, 20, 27, 28, 46–52
Compensation, 27
Control, 58–61, 161–63
Coordination, 161–63
Country Club Style, 65, 68, 69

D

Decision making, 20, 127–51
Delegation and control, 20, 28, 56–58
Documentation, 93, 96
Drucker, Peter, 2, 49, 60, 80

E

Egalitarianism, 4
80/20 rule, 87

F

Feedback on performance, 33

H

Herzberg, Frederick, 25, 26

I

Impoverished Style, 65, 67, 68, 69
Improvement of productivity, 2–3

J

Job definition, 93, 96
Job description, 35
Job design, 32
Job development, 20, 28, 29–33
Job measurement, 96

L

Leadership style, 20, 28, 61–72
Leverage of management, 5–6
Likert, Rensis, 45

M

McGregor, Douglas, 25, 62
Management by objectives, 79–101
Manager, task of, 1–9
Managerial Grid®, 65, 66
Managing subordinates, 20
Maslow, Abraham, 25
Middle of the Road Style, 67, 68, 69

Motivators, 26, 27
Mouton, Jane, 65

O

Objective setting, 20
Objectives, 81
    hierarchy of, 81–84
    management by, 79–101
Operational approach (to leadership), 63
Organization style, 20, 28, 72–76
Organizational integration, 15–16

P

Pareto's Law, 87
Parkinson's Law, 16
Participation, 26, 27
Performance appraisal, 28, 34–40
Personality trait appraisal, 35, 36
Personnel forms, 96
Peter Principle, The, 16
Problem analysis, 103–25
Problem definition, 103–25
Problem solving, 20
Productivity, definition, 6
Profit, 12
Pygmalion effect, 44–45

R

Recognition, 27
Results management methods, 28–29
Reward/punishment, 34

S

Scheduling, 161
Self-actualization, 25
Self-development, 27
Self-fulfilling prophecy, 44–46
Service industries, 4
Situational approach to leadership, 63, 74–75
Stewardship, 28
Stretch objective, 42–44
Style approach (to leadership), 63
Subordinate development, 20, 28
Subordinate management, 20, 23–40, 41–53, 55–78
Supervision, 27
Surplus, 12
Sweeney, James, 45
Sweeney's Miracle, 45
Synergism, 12
Systems approach, 11–21

T

Task Style, 65, 68, 69
Team, 75–76
Team management, 67, 68, 69
Technology, 4–5
Theory X, 25–26, 62, 65
Theory Y, 25–26, 62, 63, 65
Time management, 20, 169–86
Time wasters, 171–74
    solutions for, 175–80
Traitist approach (to leadership), 62

U

U.S. Government National Commission on Productivity and Work Quality, 56
Up the Organization, 16

V

Vertical loading, 31

W

Work, 27

Work breakdown structure, 160–61
Working papers, 93, 96

Y

Yellow Fever experiment, 107–8